CENSORSHIP

Opposing Viewpoints®

Other Books of Related Interest

Opposing Viewpoints Series

American Values
America's Children
America's Victims
Child Abuse
Civil Liberties
Culture Wars
Feminism
Homosexuality
Human Sexuality
Male/Female Roles
Mass Media
Pornography
Sexual Values
Teenage Sexuality
Violence

Current Controversies Series

Ethics
Family Violence
Free Speech
Hate Crimes
The Information Highway
Sexual Harassment
Violence Against Women
Violence in the Media

CENSORSHIP
Opposing Viewpoints®

David Bender & Bruno Leone, *Series Editors*

Byron L. Stay, Professor of Rhetoric and
Writing and Associate Dean at
Mount St. Mary's College, Emmitsburg,
Maryland, *Book Editor*

OPPOSING
VIEWPOINTS®
SERIES

Greenhaven Press, Inc., San Diego, CA

Photo credit: Image Club

Greenhaven Press, Inc.
PO Box 289009
San Diego, CA 92198-9009

Library of Congress Cataloging-in-Publication Data

Censorship : opposing viewpoints / Byron L. Stay, book editor.
    p.   cm. — (Opposing viewpoints series)
   Includes bibliographical references (p.   ) and index.
   ISBN 1-56510-507-9 (pbk. : alk. paper). —
ISBN 1-56510-508-7 (lib. bdg. : alk. paper)
   1. Censorship—United States. I. Title. II. Series:
Opposing viewpoints series (Unnumbered)
Z658.U5S72   1997
363.3'1'0973—dc20   96-29030
                                       CIP

"Congress shall make no law . . . abridging the freedom of speech, or of the press."

First Amendment to the U.S. Constitution

The basic foundation of our democracy is the First Amendment guarantee of freedom of expression. The Opposing Viewpoints Series is dedicated to the concept of this basic freedom and the idea that it is more important to practice it than to enshrine it.

Contents

Why Consider Opposing Viewpoints?

"The only way in which a human being can make some approach to knowing the whole of a subject is by hearing what can be said about it by persons of every variety of opinion and studying all modes in which it can be looked at by every character of mind. No wise man ever acquired his wisdom in any mode but this."

John Stuart Mill

In our media-intensive culture it is not difficult to find differing opinions. Thousands of newspapers and magazines and dozens of radio and television talk shows resound with differing points of view. The difficulty lies in deciding which opinion to agree with and which "experts" seem the most credible. The more inundated we become with differing opinions and claims, the more essential it is to hone critical reading and thinking skills to evaluate these ideas. Opposing Viewpoints books address this problem directly by presenting stimulating debates that can be used to enhance and teach these skills. The varied opinions contained in each book examine many different aspects of a single issue. While examining these conveniently edited opposing views, readers can develop critical thinking skills such as the ability to compare and contrast authors' credibility, facts, argumentation styles, use of persuasive techniques, and other stylistic tools. In short, the Opposing Viewpoints Series is an ideal way to attain the higher-level thinking and reading skills so essential in a culture of diverse and contradictory opinions.

In addition to providing a tool for critical thinking, Opposing Viewpoints books challenge readers to question their own strongly held opinions and assumptions. Most people form their opinions on the basis of upbringing, peer pressure, and personal, cultural, or professional bias. By reading carefully balanced opposing views, readers must directly confront new ideas as well as the opinions of those with whom they disagree. This is not to simplistically argue that everyone who reads opposing views will—or should—change his or her opinion. Instead, the series enhances readers' depth of understanding of their own views by encouraging confrontation with opposing ideas. Careful examination of others' views can lead to the readers' understanding of the logical inconsistencies in their own opinions, perspective on why they hold an opinion, and the consideration of the possibility that their opinion requires further evaluation.

Evaluating Other Opinions

To ensure that this type of examination occurs, Opposing Viewpoints books present all types of opinions. Prominent spokespeople on different sides of each issue as well as well-known professionals from many disciplines challenge the reader. An additional goal of the series is to provide a forum for other, less known, or even unpopular viewpoints. The opinion of an ordinary person who has had to make the decision to cut off life support from a terminally ill relative, for example, may be just as valuable and provide just as much insight as a medical ethicist's professional opinion. The editors have two additional purposes in including these less known views. One, the editors encourage readers to respect others' opinions—even when not enhanced by professional credibility. It is only by reading or listening to and objectively evaluating others' ideas that one can determine whether they are worthy of consideration. Two, the inclusion of such viewpoints encourages the important critical thinking skill of objectively evaluating an author's credentials and bias. This evaluation will illuminate an author's reasons for taking a particular stance on an issue and will aid in readers' evaluation of the author's ideas.

As series editors of the Opposing Viewpoints Series, it is our hope that these books will give readers a deeper understanding of the issues debated and an appreciation of the complexity of even seemingly simple issues when good and honest people disagree. This awareness is particularly important in a democratic society such as ours in which people enter into public debate to determine the common good. Those with whom one disagrees should not be regarded as enemies but rather as people whose views deserve careful examination and may shed light on one's own.

Thomas Jefferson once said that "difference of opinion leads to inquiry, and inquiry to truth." Jefferson, a broadly educated man, argued that "if a nation expects to be ignorant and free . . . it expects what never was and never will be." As individuals and as a nation, it is imperative that we consider the opinions of others and examine them with skill and discernment. The Opposing Viewpoints Series is intended to help readers achieve this goal.

David L. Bender & Bruno Leone,
Series Editors

Introduction

"Congress shall make no law . . . abridging the freedom of speech, or of the press."
—from the First Amendment to the U.S. Constitution

Since the nation's founding, freedom of speech has been an important part of American democracy. Democracy is based on the idea that only when people are free to express their views openly can they govern themselves effectively. In addition, it is commonly assumed that when citizens feel as though they can assemble peacefully and criticize their government without censure, they will be less likely to resort to violence and revolt. Thus, freedom of speech—and freedom from censorship—is not only considered necessary for a democracy to function, it is also believed to help protect governments against threats from within.

The framers of the Constitution were well aware of these advantages to freedom of speech in 1791 when they drafted the Bill of Rights—especially when they drafted the First Amendment. However, while freedom of speech has long been a cherished American ideal, in practice no government can condone all forms of speech. Since 1791 there have been numerous attempts (with varying degrees of success) to limit free speech—including speech that threatens the national interest, speech with a potential to incite injurious behavior, speech that infringes on the rights of others, and extreme kinds of pornography and obscenity. Conversely, over the years the concept of freedom of speech has been expanded to include not just spoken or written work but also symbolic acts of expression such as wearing black armbands, publishing pictures and artworks, and flag burning.

Few reasonable people are likely to disagree about the need to limit extreme kinds of damaging speech, such as yelling "fire" in a theater or exposing children to material that is clearly obscene. However, drawing the line between what is obscene and what is innocuous, what is art and what is pornography, can be difficult. In the twentieth century, individuals and groups have often disagreed about what types of speech should and should not be censored. Censorship battles have been waged over publicly funded art, violence in the media, pornography, and other forms of expression.

One area of controversy concerns the method of determining what books students should have access to in public schools. Many free speech proponents maintain that censorship, in the form of book banning, is at work in the schools. Organizations such as the American Library Association (ALA) and People For the American Way (PFAW), among others, insist that many books are being banned by conservative Christian school boards and parents. In most cases of school book banning, according to the ALA and PFAW, books are singled out and excluded because they are thought to contradict Christian values and beliefs. For example, many people have objected to the presence of the books *Daddy's Roommate* and *Heather Has Two Mommies* in school libraries because they disagree with the books' positive presentation of homosexuality.

Others insist that books are not being banned from public schools. Those who disagree with the ALA and the PAW point out that each year thousands of books are published that could be used in public schools. Because only a fraction of these books can be purchased by schools, some books must necessarily be excluded. The decision to reject one book in favor of another, these commentators argue, is not an act of censorship but a decision by parents and school boards about what information is appropriate for the age level of the students in question. As conservative columnist Cal Thomas writes, "The ALA counts as book-banning efforts by parents to become involved in their children's education by raising questions concerning age-appropriate material." Thomas and others believe that it is appropriate for parents to make the decisions about what educational materials their children have access to.

Decisions concerning what constitutes censorship are often difficult, as are decisions about what should and should not be censored. These difficulties are addressed by the authors included in *Censorship: Opposing Viewpoints*. This anthology, which replaces Greenhaven's 1990 volume of the same title, contains the following chapters: Should There Be Limits to Free Speech? Is Censorship Occurring in Schools and Libraries? Are Stronger Antipornography Laws Needed? Should the Entertainment Media Be Censored? Throughout these chapters, authors debate which types of speech are protected by the First Amendment and which should be curtailed.

Should There Be Limits to Free Speech?

CENSORSHIP

Chapter Preface

Ever since the ratification of the Bill of Rights, which includes the First Amendment guarantee of free speech, the issue of whether or not unfettered speech should be allowed has been debated repeatedly. While the free expression of words and ideas is a celebrated American ideal, such expression is occasionally perceived as posing a threat to society. Some Americans support restrictions on specific types of speech because they believe the potential harm of such expression outweighs its benefits.

Many people, for instance, argue that an absolute right to free speech should not extend to those who produce pornographic or violent material. Believing that violent and sexually explicit words and images can encourage people to commit acts of violence, critics advocate restrictions on the production and distribution of pornography, films, and music, as well as on the broadcasting of violent television shows. For example, arguing against extending First Amendment rights to pornography, feminist Catharine MacKinnon states that "buying and selling women and children is no one's civil liberty."

Opponents of censorship argue that any restriction of speech— even speech full of violence and hate—is a greater threat to society than that posed by potentially harmful expressions. For example, many feminists contend that when censorship of pornography is permitted, one segment of society (the censors) is placed in a position to dictate what types of sexual expression are acceptable for everyone, thereby threatening women's freedom to control their own sexuality. For this reason, Leonore Tiefer, a psychologist and an associate professor at Montefiore Medical Center in New York, insists that "women are in more danger from the repression of sexually-explicit material than from its expression."

Pornography is just one form of expression that is targeted for censorship. Other types of speech that have been singled out as harmful include offensive works of art, derogatory speech aimed at minorities and women ("hate speech"), and the burning of the American flag (which many people consider to be an act of symbolic speech). Whether these and other forms of speech should be subject to restrictions is examined in the following chapter.

"Censorship as such is an appropriate exercise of government power."

Censorship Can Be Beneficial

Thomas Storck

In the following viewpoint, Thomas Storck examines various arguments against censorship and finds them to be unpersuasive. Storck argues that some ideas lead to harmful actions, and that the government should censor such ideas in order to protect the community. Storck, a librarian in Washington, D.C., insists that censorship can both prevent harmful acts and facilitate society's intellectual pursuit of truth.

As you read, consider the following questions:

1. How does the author define censorship?
2. What evil acts does the author believe can be prevented by censorship?
3. According to Storck, why will censorship not hinder the search for truth?

Thomas Storck, "A Case for Censorship," *New Oxford Review*, May 1996. Copyright ©1996 New Oxford Review. Reprinted with permission from the author and *New Oxford Review* (1069 Kains Ave., Berkeley, CA 94706).

Anyone currently undertaking to defend censorship has to reckon not only with considerable abhorrence of the practice, but even with distaste for the word itself. It seems that even those who would like to restrict publications, broadcasts, or films shy away from the term "censorship." They are at pains to distinguish what they would do from what censors do. When the head of the National Coalition on Television Violence testified before Congress in December 1992 and presented a "10-point plan to sweep violence off TV and off our streets," it is interesting that the first point in the plan was "no censorship." No one wants to own up to being a would-be censor, and thus very few are willing to stand up and openly defend this venerable practice. But I am happy to do so, for censorship has long seemed to me a necessary, if regrettable, part of practical political wisdom and an opportunity for the judicious exercise of human intelligence. For, human nature being what it is, it is naive to think we can freely read and view things that promote or portray evil deeds without sometimes feeling encouraged to commit such deeds. And if this is the case, then censorship can sometimes be a necessity.

Defining Censorship

But before defending censorship I need to define it. And I define censorship simply as the restriction, absolute or merely to some part of the population (e.g., to the unlearned or to children), by the proper political authorities, of intellectual, literary, or artistic material in any format. I want to note two things especially about this definition. First, I am not talking simply about censoring pornography. I also include censorship of works that are expressions of erroneous *ideas*, a position which I realize is extremely unpopular today, even more hated than the banning of obscene works. Secondly, I am concerned only with censorship by governments. The determination of intellectual or cultural matters for the sake of the common good, such as what books and other things the nation may read or view, is not properly the work of private pressure groups or crusading individuals, though their work may sometimes be necessary when the state does not carry out its proper functions in this area. But the state alone has general care of the temporal common good, and censorship is one of the most important ways of safeguarding that good.

I am concerned here only with censorship in the abstract. That is, I am not defending or advocating any particular act of censorship in the past, present, or future, or in any particular country or legal system, though I do need to offer some hypothetical examples. I am simply arguing that there is nothing intrinsically wrong with censoring. All I hope to achieve is to

18

make a compelling case that censorship *as such* is an appropriate exercise of governmental power and that the practical difficulties necessarily involved, while great, are not overwhelming.

Since I am speaking of censorship in the abstract, considerations based on the First Amendment to the U.S. Constitution or on decisions of the U.S. Supreme Court are not relevant to my argument. Whatever restrictions the American Constitution wisely or unwisely imposes on governmental power with respect to freedom of expression do not apply to governments *in general*.

Protecting the Community

What then is the case that can be made for censorship? It can be stated in the following simple thesis: Ideas lead to actions, and bad ideas often lead to bad acts, bringing harm to individuals and possible ruin to societies. Just as the state has the right to restrict and direct a person's actions when he is a physical threat to the community, so also in the matter of intellectual or cultural threats, the authorities have duties to protect the community.

It is obviously necessary for me to explain and defend these assertions, and the place to begin is with a discussion of the question of whether we can actually identify good and evil. I said above that "bad ideas often lead to bad acts," but if we cannot identify what is the bad, then clearly we cannot know either bad ideas or bad acts. One problem in discussions of whether we can know good and evil is the assumption that we either know all good and evil or we know none. It seems sometimes to be assumed that proponents of censorship are claiming to know good and evil exhaustively, that they know the moral status of everything that exists. But this is not the case. If we knew with certainty that, say, only one thing was evil, and if that evil were great enough and threatened society enough, then we might well decide to censor expressions and advocacy of that one thing, regardless of how ignorant we were about other moral questions.

Can we actually know any evils? I think each reader already knows or thinks he knows many more than one. So I will select an instance of evil—rape. I suspect that all readers would readily say that rape is clearly an evil. And an evil not because they think so, but an evil in and of itself. Not an evil because most people or most thinkers condemn it, but an evil independently of what other people might believe. If this is the case, then human beings *can* know with certainty at least one example of evil.

Encouraging Evil

Now here is an example of something I think most people would agree was not only evil, but likely to encourage evil conduct. I have read that at some time during the 1970s there were billboards in Los Angeles and perhaps elsewhere advertising a Rolling

Stones album which showed a pretty woman with bruises—black and blue marks—with the legend, "I'm black and blue from the Rolling Stones and I love it." Abuse of women is an evil, and the not too subtle encouragement given to the practice, by insinuating that women really want to be abused, seems to me an almost textbook example of the need for censorship.

To return to my first example, suppose someone wrote a book arguing that women really want to be raped, that they enjoy it, and that men do them a favor by raping them. Suppose, in addition, the book maintained that rape is the best sex going and the best way to prove one's masculinity—including, by way of an appendix, statistics on how few rapists get caught and the light sentences often given. Now rape, I think we agreed above, is clearly an evil. Would anyone argue that such a book would not promote rapes? Even if it were true that many men would not be affected by such a book, nevertheless can we confidently say that such a book would not be responsible for rapes? Do we want to remove whatever inhibitions there may be that restrain even one potential rapist?

Creating Violence with Speech

It is relatively easy to create conditions of physical harm to oneself or to others through the use of speech. Should a speaker make statements that are designed to create immediate bodily harm to another person or other persons, then civility breaks down. One might also speak to another in such a way that the speaker's physical self is in danger. . . .

To call for someone's annihilation by violence or to incite someone by using abusive, vile, or profane language that violates a person's cultural and social existence and/or the sanctity of the person's life, though not violent itself, could conceivably create a condition of violence.

Molefi Kete Asante, *National Forum*, Spring 1995.

Now if we can identify certain evils, and if advocacy of those evils seems likely to encourage people to commit them, then why should we not take the next and logical step and prohibit such advocacy? If to commit certain evils is harmful to others and a crime, then why should advocating and encouraging such evils be perfectly lawful? Must a community be unable to protect itself? Must the authorities be helpless to restrain the source of the evil?

This constitutes the best case that can be made for censorship. But in most people's minds the case *against* censorship looms much larger than any assent to this argument. It looms so much larger that in effect the real case for censorship is largely the removal of people's overwhelming fears of censorship. Most people's objections to censorship are based on fear. So with this in mind, I will discuss the chief *objections* to censorship.

The most fundamental objection, already touched on above, is to deny that we know with certainty any goods or any evils. If this were true, then in practicing censorship we would be just as likely to restrain some newfound truth as to protect society from some dangerous evil. And though this professed ignorance of good and evil is popular today, the only people who can consistently make such an argument are those who are not advocates of anything at all. I have never met any of them. Many may profess moral skepticism in a broad philosophical sense, but they are often the most passionate defenders of this or that cause or opinion. How they reconcile this with their supposed skepticism, if they even try, I do not know.

The argument from skepticism is put very forcefully by John Stuart Mill's *On Liberty*. But those who hold this opinion, and who argue most passionately against censorship on the grounds of our lack of certainty of good and evil, must face the fact that every time society makes a law it is making a judgment of good and evil. If some street thug had stolen Mill's hat, and when he demanded it back the policeman and magistrate replied that for all they knew private property might be immoral and therefore they could not compel the thief to return the hat, Mill might have been more than a little annoyed. Yet to support the punishment of thieves while allowing the publication of books advocating theft—on the ground that we do not know whether theft is right or wrong—seems a trifle inconsistent and even hypocritical.

Bad Ideas Lead to Bad Action

Another objection is to deny that there is a connection between advocacy of evil and any actual instances of evil. But even among those who tend to oppose censorship, there is a recognition that ideas lead to action and bad ideas lead to bad action. For example, many liberally-minded people attempt to prevent their children, and everyone else's too, from reading books that perpetuate what they consider sexual stereotypes. They believe they have identified an instance of evil, "sexual stereotyping," and that reading books that promote it or take it for granted will tend to form "sexist" individuals who in turn will commit "sexist" acts. Regardless of whether one regards "sexual stereotypes" as evil, and regardless of whether one regards such liberally-minded people as in fact illiberal, this position is certainly a coherent one. It is easy to understand why such people do not want children reading books that contain

21

what they consider to be evil. They have made the obvious judgment that writings tend to influence action, and almost all of us would understand such a judgment, even if we disagree with their application of that judgment in this particular case.

Take a couple different examples: How many of us would think that it would be of no consequence were the Ku Klux Klan or the neo-Nazis to own half the newspapers and television networks in the country? Or how many of us wouldn't mind if our children were regularly taught by outspoken racists in the schools? Indeed, if ideas expressed in written or spoken word do not lead men to act, then why does every political, religious, philosophical, or cultural group or movement attempt to persuade us by the written and spoken word how to live and act? And why are millions of dollars spent on commercial advertising?

Censorship in Practice

Perhaps few will now be bold—or illogical—enough to attack censorship on either of the above grounds. But there are two other arguments against censorship. The first is that whatever the formal case in favor of censorship, in actual practice censors have always stifled creativity and hindered the discovery of truth, so that whatever danger there is to society from the advocacy of evil, much more harm will result from the always stupid—and in some cases malicious—actions of the censors themselves.

Strictly speaking, this argument is not opposed to the state's right to censor. It simply says that since we will always or nearly always do it unintelligently, it would be much better not to do it at all. Some of those who would argue thus might even admit the (purely theoretical) point that were there someone endowed with superhuman intelligence, knowledge, wisdom, and probity, it might be safe to allow him to be the censor. But never anyone else. Although I am arguing for censorship in the abstract, I *am* thinking of the world as it actually is. And though I willingly admit that many instances of censorship by individuals and pressure groups have been stupid or perverse, still I believe that in a society fully committed to its practice, censorship can be carried on no more foolishly than we manage the rest of human affairs. Restrictions on books, films, or broadcasts always carry some danger. To give fallible men the power to decide what we can read or view or hear will surely sometimes allow excesses and even outrages. But so does giving some men the power to arrest or to punish. The question is: Is an activity necessary enough that we will accept inevitable abuses for the sake of the good that needs to be done? We make some men policemen and give them guns and the right to arrest others and even in some cases the right to use deadly force. Obviously there have been and will be abuses. But most of us do not advocate

22

doing away with the police, even though they sometimes shoot and *kill* innocent people. Instead, things such as more and better education for policemen and more and clearer guidelines for use of force or of arrest are usually suggested. I would say similar things about censors. The ideal censor is not some ill-educated, parochial bigot, but someone of liberal education and continued wide reading, someone with a grasp of first principles and enough experience and wisdom to see how they should be put into practice. Of course, even then our censors will make mistakes. As in all legal matters, there must be room for reconsideration and appeal. But if we know that something is evil, and see that its advocacy is likely to bring about or increase actual evil acts, then to do nothing because we anticipate that censors will sometimes err is not a responsible position to take. Those who think that, with censorship, literature and creativity will dry up, forget that most of the great works of the past, up to and in some cases beyond the 19th century, were produced under government or ecclesiastical censorship. When we think of a society in which censorship is practiced, we should think of the one that produced Shakespeare's plays or Cervantes's *Don Quixote*, not of the Bible Belt's narrow provincialism or the tyrannies of Hitler or Stalin. Censors need not be ignorant fanatics.

Suppressing Error

The other argument commonly made against censorship is this: That in the free play of ideas, truth will ultimately and necessarily triumph. Censorship, therefore, is at best unnecessary and at worst a hindrance to the discovery of truth. Strictly speaking, this argument is really not against censorship, and when examined carefully will actually be found to support it. For even if it is the case that truth will always emerge from the give and take of free debate (a questionable proposition), how can the suppression of evident error harm that process? If a number of assertions are competing for acceptance, and (let us say) we know that two of them are false, how can removing those two from the debate make it harder for the truth to be discerned among the rest? Surely by narrowing the field and leaving us more time to examine those theories that might be true, we have made it even more likely that the truth will be found in our free examination of conflicting ideas. Moreover, most of those who make the claim that truth will always emerge from totally free debate are not really interested in discovering truths. They simply use this argument to foster a climate in which relativism flourishes and mankind is perpetually in doubt about truth and error, right and wrong.

A final point that must be noted is the connection between anti-censorship arguments and the free market. Both glorify indi-

vidualism at the expense of the common good, and the rich at the expense of the poor. It is primarily the rich who promote and subsidize ideas and art that undermine traditional ways of life, and it is primarily the poor who suffer on that account. Society exists to protect and promote the welfare of all, but especially of the poor and the workingman. To exalt the free and irresponsible expression of the individual is to take up a position contrary to the community's duty of protecting the poor. Only those with sufficient money and ennui have the time or resources to produce ideas or art that corrupt or debase. Censorship is a protection of the poor from the acting out of the perverted fantasies of the rich, from the Marquis de Sade to Leopold and Loeb. Who benefits today from the continuing corruption of the public by movies, television, and music filled with sex and violence? Studio owners, directors, actors, and suchlike. Like unfettered capitalism, complete freedom of expression is simply a means by which those with money and influence remake society at the expense of those without these things.

This, I think, is what can be said on behalf of censorship. Our opposition to it is largely based on fear and the emotional effects of slogans. If we could free our minds, we might be able to consider the case for censorship and see that it has merit. That there is no consensus today about what is right and wrong does not disprove what I have said. For though now we could never actually produce a censorship code that commanded a consensus of support, yet we can still recognize in the abstract that censorship is a legitimate practice. It never hurts to order our thoughts correctly, even if we cannot just now put them into practice.

"In free societies, you must have the free play of ideas."

Censorship Is Harmful

Salman Rushdie and Jonathan Rauch

Salman Rushdie is the author of *The Satanic Verses*, a novel that was deemed blasphemous by the Islamic government of Iran. He has been in hiding since February 1989, when the Ayatollah Khomeini of Iran issued a decree calling for his death. In Part I of the following viewpoint, which is excerpted from a speech he delivered to the American Society of Newspaper Editors, Rushdie argues that an essential element of a free society is the uncensored competition among opposing ideas and beliefs. In Part II, Jonathan Rauch maintains that in order to ensure freedom of speech, even expressions of racism, sexism, and other forms of prejudice must be permitted free play. Rauch is a writer for the *Economist* and the author of *Kindly Inquisitors: The New Attacks on Free Thought*.

As you read, consider the following questions:

1. How has the concept of "respect" been distorted, in Rushdie's opinion?
2. Why is the elimination of prejudice an impossible undertaking, according to Rauch?
3. Why should minorities oppose the effort to rid society of prejudice, in Rauch's opinion?

I

In any vision of a free society, the value of free speech must rank the highest, for that is the freedom without which all the other freedoms would fail. Journalists do more than most of us to protect those values, for the exercise of freedom is freedom's best defense, and that is something you all do every day.

A Censorious Age

It seems to me, however, that we live in an increasingly censorious age. By this I mean that the broad, indeed international, acceptance of 1st Amendment principles is being steadily eroded. Many special-interest groups, claiming the moral high ground, now demand the protection of the censor. Political correctness and the rise of the religious right provide the pro-censorship lobby with further cohorts. I would like to say a little about just one of the weapons of this resurgent lobby, a weapon used, interestingly, by everyone from antipornography feminists to religious fundamentalists: I mean the concept of "respect."

Respect

On the surface of it, "respect" is one of those ideas nobody's against. Like a good warm coat in winter, like applause, like ketchup on your fries, everybody wants some of that. Sock-it-to-me-sock-it-to-me, as Aretha Franklin has it. But what we used to mean by respect—what Aretha meant by it—that is, a mixture of good-hearted consideration and serious attention—has little to do with the new ideological usage of the word.

Religious extremists demand respect for their attitudes with growing stridency. Very few people would object to the idea that people's rights to religious belief must be respected—after all, the 1st Amendment defends those rights as unequivocally as it defends free speech—but now we are asked to agree that to dissent from those beliefs—to hold that they are suspect or antiquated or wrong—that, in fact, they are arguable—is incompatible with the idea of respect. When criticism is placed off limits as "disrespectful" and therefore offensive, something strange is happening to the concept of respect. Yet in recent times, both the U.S. National Endowment for the Arts and the British Broadcasting Corp. have announced that they will use this new version of "respect" as a touchstone for their funding and programming decisions.

Other minority groups—racial, sexual, social—also have demanded that they be accorded this new form of respect. To "respect" Louis Farrakhan, we must understand, is simply to agree with him. To "diss" him is, equally simply, to disagree. But if dissent is also to be thought a form of "dissing," then we have indeed succumbed to the Thought Police.

26

I want to suggest to you that citizens of free societies, democracies, do not preserve their freedom by pussyfooting around their fellow citizens' opinions, even their most cherished beliefs. In free societies, you must have the free play of ideas. There must be argument, and it must be impassioned and untrammeled. A free society is not a calm and eventless place—that is the kind of static, dead society dictators try to create. Free societies are dynamic, noisy, turbulent and full of radical disagreements. Skepticism and freedom are indissolubly linked. And it is the skepticism of journalists, their show-me, prove-it unwillingness to be impressed, that is perhaps their most important contribution to the freedom of the free world.

It is the disrespect of journalists—for power, for orthodoxy, for party lines, for ideologies, for vanity, for arrogance, for folly, for pretension, for corruption, for stupidity, maybe even for editors—that I would like to celebrate and that I urge you all, in freedom's name, to preserve.

II

The war on prejudice is now, in all likelihood, the most uncontroversial social movement in America. Opposition to "hate speech," formerly identified with the liberal left, has become a bipartisan piety. Groups and factions that agree on nothing else have agreed that the public expression of any and all prejudices must be forbidden. On the left, protesters and editorialists have insisted that Francis L. Lawrence resign as president of Rutgers University for describing blacks as "a disadvantaged population that doesn't have that genetic, hereditary background to have a higher average." On the other side of the ideological divide, Ralph Reed, the executive director of the Christian Coalition, responded to criticism of the religious right by calling a press conference to denounce a supposed outbreak of "name-calling, scapegoating, and religious bigotry." Craig Rogers, an evangelical Christian student at California State University, recently filed a $2.5 million sexual-harassment suit against a lesbian professor of psychology, claiming that anti-male bias in one of her lectures violated campus rules and left him feeling "raped and trapped."

A Sweet Dream

In universities and on Capitol Hill, in workplaces and newsrooms, authorities are declaring that there is no place for racism, sexism, homophobia, Christian-bashing, and other forms of prejudice in public debate or even in private thought. "Only when racism and other forms of prejudice are expunged," say the crusaders for sweetness and light, "can minorities be safe and society be fair." So sweet, this dream of a world without prejudice. But the very last thing society should do is seek to utterly eradicate racism and other forms of prejudice.

I suppose I should say, in the customary I-hope-I-don't-sound-too-defensive tone, that I am not a racist and that this is not a viewpoint favoring racism or any other particular prejudice. It is a viewpoint favoring intellectual pluralism, which permits the expression of various forms of bigotry and always will. Although we like to hope that a time will come when no one will believe that people come in types and that each type belongs with its own kind, I doubt such a day will ever arrive. By all indications, *Homo sapiens* is a tribal species for whom "us versus them" comes naturally and must be continually pushed back. Where there is genuine freedom of expression, there will be racist expression. There will also be people who believe that homosexuals are sick or threaten children or—especially among teenagers—are rightful targets of manly savagery. Homosexuality will always be incomprehensible to most people, and what is incomprehensible is feared. As for anti-Semitism, it appears to be a hardier virus than influenza. If you want pluralism, then you get racism and sexism and homophobia, and communism and fascism and xenophobia and tribalism, and that is just for a start. If you want to believe in intellectual freedom and the progress of knowledge and the advancement of science and all those other good things, then you must swallow hard and accept this: for as thickheaded and wayward an animal as us, the realistic question is how to make the best of prejudice, not how to eradicate it.

A Meaningless Proposition

Indeed, "eradicating prejudice" is so vague a proposition as to be meaningless. Distinguishing prejudice reliably and nonpolitically from non-prejudice, or even defining it crisply, is quite hopeless. We all feel we know prejudice when we see it. But do we? At the University of Michigan, a student said in a classroom discussion that he considered homosexuality a disease treatable with therapy. He was summoned to a formal disciplinary hearing for violating the school's policy against speech that "victimizes" people based on "sexual orientation." Now, the evidence is abundant that this particular hypothesis is wrong, and any American homosexual can attest to the harm that the student's hypothesis has inflicted on many real people. But was it a statement of prejudice or of misguided belief? Hate speech or hypothesis? Many Americans who do not regard themselves as bigots or haters believe that homosexuality is a treatable disease. They may be wrong, but are they all bigots? I am unwilling to say so, and if you are willing, beware. The line between a prejudiced belief and a merely controversial one is elusive, and the harder you look the more elusive it becomes. "God hates ho-

mosexuals" is a statement of fact, not of bias, to those who believe it; "American criminals are disproportionately black" is a
statement of bias, not of fact, to those who disbelieve it.

Who is right? You may decide, and so may others, and there is
no need to agree. That is the great innovation of intellectual pluralism (which is to say, of post-Enlightenment science, broadly
defined). We cannot know in advance or for sure which belief is
prejudice and which is truth, but to advance knowledge we
don't need to know. The genius of intellectual pluralism lies not
in doing away with prejudices and dogmas but in channeling
them—making them socially productive by pitting prejudice
against prejudice and dogma against dogma, exposing all to
withering public criticism. What survives at the end of the day
is our base of knowledge. . . .

Purism

The sweeping implications of this challenge to pluralism are
not, I think, well enough understood by the public at large. Indeed, the new brand of totalism has yet even to be properly
named. "Multiculturalism," for instance, is much too broad. "Political correctness" comes closer but is too trendy and snide. For
lack of anything else, I will call the new antipluralism "purism,"
since its major tenet is that society cannot be just until the last
traces of invidious prejudice have been scrubbed away. Whatever you call it, the purists' way of seeing things has spread
through American intellectual life with remarkable speed, so
much so that many people will blink at you uncomprehendingly
or even call you a racist (or sexist or homophobe, etc.) if you
suggest that expressions of racism should be tolerated or that
prejudice has its part to play.

The new purism sets out, to begin with, on a campaign against
words, for words are the currency of prejudice, and if prejudice
is hurtful then so must be prejudiced words. "We are not safe
when these violent words are among us," wrote Mari Matsuda,
then a UCLA law professor. Here one imagines gangs of racist
words swinging chains and smashing heads in back alleys. To
suppress bigoted language seems, at first blush, reasonable, but
it quickly leads to a curious result. A peculiar kind of verbal
shamanism takes root, as though certain expressions, like curses
or magical incantations, carry in themselves the power to hurt
or heal—as though words were bigoted rather than people.
"Context is everything," people have always said. The use of the
word "nigger" in *Huckleberry Finn* does not make the book an
"act" of hate speech—or does it? In the new view, this is no
longer so clear. The very utterance of the word "nigger" (at least
by a non-black) is a racist act. When a *Sacramento Bee* cartoonist
put the word "nigger" mockingly in the mouth of a white su-

premacist, there were howls of protest and 1,400 canceled subscriptions and an editorial apology, even though the word was plainly being invoked against racists, not against blacks.

Faced with escalating demands of verbal absolutism, newspapers issue lists of forbidden words. The expressions "gyp" (derived from "Gypsy") and "Dutch treat" were among the dozens of terms stricken as "offensive" in a much-ridiculed (and later withdrawn) *Los Angeles Times* speech code. The University of Missouri journalism school issued a *Dictionary of Cautionary Words and Phrases*, which included "*Buxom:* Offensive reference to a woman's chest. Do not use. See 'Woman.' *Codger:* Offensive reference to a senior citizen."

The Answer Is More Speech

Acknowledging the freedom of conscience that the First Amendment requires us to accept is one thing; actually living with it is quite another. When someone is speaking what we consider blasphemy or disrespect for the flag, our first impulse may be to punch him in the nose, our second is to seek a law that will prevent his behavior. The First Amendment requires just the opposite. It requires us to protect the *right* of the person uttering such words, but it does not require us to agree. In fact, the answer to vicious or wrongheaded speech is always more speech, compelling speech, persuasive speech. The greatest abdication of our duty as citizens is to remain silent in the face of hateful, degrading speech.

John Frohnmayer, *Out of Tune: Listening to the First Amendment*, 1995.

As was bound to happen, purists soon discovered that chasing around after words like "gyp" or "buxom" hardly goes to the roots of the problem. As long as they remain bigoted, bigots will simply find other words. If they can't call you a kike then they will say Jewboy, Judas, or Hebe, and when all those are banned they will press words like "oven" and "lampshade" into their service. The vocabulary of hate is potentially as rich as your dictionary, and all you do by banning language used by cretins is to let them decide what the rest of us may say. The problem, some purists have concluded, must therefore go much deeper than laws: it must go to the deeper level of ideas. Racism, sexism, homophobia, and the rest must be built into the very structure of American society and American patterns of thought, so pervasive yet so insidious that, like water to a fish, they are both omnipresent and unseen. The mere existence of prejudice constructs a society whose very nature is prejudiced.

This line of thinking was pioneered by feminists, who argued that pornography, more than just being expressive, is an act by which men construct an oppressive society. Racial activists quickly picked up the argument. Racist expressions are themselves acts of oppression, they said. "All racist speech constructs the social reality that constrains the liberty of nonwhites because of their race," wrote Charles R. Lawrence III, then a law professor at Stanford. From the purist point of view, a society with even one racist is a racist society, because the idea itself threatens and demeans its targets. They cannot feel wholly safe or wholly welcome as long as racism is present. Pluralism says: There will always be some racists. Marginalize them, ignore them, exploit them, ridicule them, take pains to make their policies illegal, but otherwise leave them alone. Purists say: That's not enough. Society cannot be just until these pervasive and oppressive ideas are searched out and eradicated. . . .

The purist campaign reaches, in the end, into the mind itself. In a lecture at the University of New Hampshire, a professor compared writing to sex ("You and the subject become one"); he was suspended and required to apologize, but what was most insidious was the order to undergo university-approved counseling to have his mind straightened out. At the University of Pennsylvania, a law lecturer said, "We have ex-slaves here who should know about the Thirteenth Amendment"; he was banished from campus for a year and required to make a public apology, and he, too, was compelled to attend a "sensitivity and racial awareness" session. Mandatory re-education of alleged bigots is the natural consequence of intellectual purism. Prejudice must be eliminated! . . .

Minority Voices

What is especially dismaying is that the purists pursue prejudice in the name of protecting minorities. In order to protect people like me (homosexual), they must pursue people like me (dissident). In order to bolster minority self-esteem, they suppress minority opinion. There are, of course, all kinds of practical and legal problems with the purists' campaign: the incursions against the First Amendment; the inevitable abuses by prosecutors and activists who define as "hateful" or "violent" whatever speech they dislike or can score points off of; the lack of any evidence that repressing prejudice eliminates rather than inflames it. But minorities, of all people, ought to remember that by definition we cannot prevail by numbers, and we generally cannot prevail by force. Against the power of ignorant mass opinion and group prejudice and superstition, we have only our voices. If you doubt that minorities' voices are powerful weapons, think of the lengths to which Southern officials went to silence the Reverend Martin Luther King Jr. (recall that the city commissioner of Montgomery, Alabama, won a $500,000 libel suit, later overturned in *New York Times* v. *Sullivan* [1964], regarding an advertisement in the *Times* placed by civil-rights leaders who denounced the Montgomery police). Think of how much gay people have improved their lot over twenty-five years simply by refusing to remain silent. Recall the Michigan student who was prosecuted for saying that homosexuality is a treatable disease, and notice that he was black. Under that Michigan speech code, more than twenty blacks were charged with racist speech, while no instance of racist speech by whites was punished. In Florida, the hate-speech law was invoked against a black man who called a policeman a "white cracker"; not so surprisingly, in the first hate-crimes case to reach the Supreme Court, the victim was white and the defendant black.

In the escalating war against "prejudice," the right is already learning to play by the rules that were pioneered by the purist activists of the left. In 1994 leading Democrats, including the President, criticized the Republican Party for being increasingly in the thrall of the Christian right. Some of the rhetoric was harsh ("fire-breathing Christian radical right"), but it wasn't vicious or even clearly wrong. Never mind: when Democratic Representative Vic Fazio said Republicans were "being forced to the fringes by the aggressive political tactics of the religious right," the chairman of the Republican National Committee, Haley Barbour, said, "Christian-bashing" was "the left's preferred form of religious bigotry." Bigotry! Prejudice! "Christians active in politics are now on the receiving end of an extraordinary campaign of bias and prejudice," said the conservative leader William J. Bennett. One discerns, here, where the new purism leads. Eventually, any criticism of any group will be "prejudice."

Words as Violence?

Here is the ultimate irony of the new purism: words, which pluralists hope can be substituted for violence, are redefined by purists *as* violence. "The experience of being called 'nigger,' 'spic,' 'Jap,' or 'kike' is like receiving a slap in the face," Charles Lawrence wrote in 1990. "Psychic injury is no less an injury than being struck in the face, and it often is far more severe." This kind of talk is commonplace today. Epithets, insults, often even polite expressions of what's taken to be prejudice are called by purists "assaultive speech," "words that wound," "verbal violence." "To me, racial epithets are not speech," one University of Michigan law professor said. "They are bullets." In her speech accepting the 1993 Nobel Prize for Literature in Stockholm, Sweden, the author Toni Morrison said this: "Oppressive language does more than represent violence; it is violence."

It is not violence. . . . Equating "verbal violence" with physical violence is a treacherous, mischievous business. Not long ago a writer was charged with viciously and gratuitously wounding the feelings and dignity of millions of people. He was charged, in effect, with exhibiting flagrant prejudice against Muslims and outrageously slandering their beliefs. "What is freedom of expression?" mused Salman Rushdie a year after the ayatollahs sentenced him to death and put a price on his head. "Without the freedom to offend, it ceases to exist." I can think of nothing sadder than that minority activists, in their haste to make the world better, should be the ones to forget the lesson of Rushdie's plight: for minorities, pluralism, not purism, is the answer. The campaigns to eradicate prejudice . . . should stop, now. The whole objective of eradicating prejudice, as opposed to correcting and criticizing it, should be repudiated as a fool's errand. Salman Rushdie is right, Toni Morrison wrong, and minorities belong at his side, not hers.

"Burning the flag is no more speech than vandalizing a cemetery, or scrawling slogans on a church or synagogue, or spray-painting a national monument."

Flag Burning Should Be Banned

Paul Greenberg

In the following viewpoint, nationally syndicated columnist Paul Greenberg argues in favor of a proposed constitutional amendment banning desecration of the American flag. Greenberg contends that burning the flag is not a form of free speech and is therefore not protected by the First Amendment.

As you read, consider the following questions:
1. How does the author differentiate between the idea and the act of defacing the flag?
2. What are the consequences of doing nothing when the flag is desecrated, according to Greenberg?
3. What does Greenberg believe the law needs to teach American society?

The flag amendment is back. And well on its way to becoming the 28th Amendment to the Constitution of the United States. What's this? It was supposed to be dead, remember?

But on June 28, 1995, the House of Representatives voted in favor of a simple declaration that, once upon a common-sense time, would scarcely have attracted notice, let alone controversy: "The Congress and the States shall have the power to prohibit the physical desecration of the flag of the United States." The vote was 312 to 120, easily more than the two-thirds' vote (280) required to propose a constitutional amendment. The prospect for Senate approval is good, and the states are primed to ratify.

But didn't our intelligentsia explain to us yokels again and again that burning the flag of the United States isn't an action, but speech, and therefore a constitutionally protected right? That's what the Supreme Court decided, too, if only in one of its confused and confusing 5-to-4 splits.

Reflecting Public Opinion

But the people don't seem to have caught on. They still insist that burning the flag is burning the flag, not making a speech. Stubborn lot, the people. Powerful thing, public opinion. Congress certainly seems to be reflecting it.

It isn't the *idea* of desecrating the flag that the American people propose to ban. Any street-corner orator who takes a notion to should be able to stand on a soapbox and bad-mouth the American flag all day long—and apple pie and motherhood, too, if that's the way the speaker feels. It's a free country.

It's actually burning Old Glory, it's defacing the Stars and Stripes, it's the physical desecration of the flag of the United States that ought to be against the law. And the people of the United States just can't seem to be talked out of that notion—or orated out of it, or lectured out of it, or condescended and patronized out of it.

Maybe it's because the people can't shut their eyes to homely truths as easily as our Advanced Thinkers. How many legs does a dog have, Abraham Lincoln once asked, if you call its tail a leg? And he answered: still four. Calling a tail a leg doesn't make it one. Not even a symbolic leg. The people have this stubborn notion that calling something a constitutional right doesn't make it one, despite the best our theorists and pettifoggers can do.

Symbols and Presences

The people keep being told that their flag is just a symbol.
Just a symbol.
"We live by symbols," said a justice of the United States

Supreme Court (Felix Frankfurter) when the standards for appointees, whether liberals or conservatives or neither, were considerably higher. And if a nation lives by its symbols, it also dies with them.

To turn aside when the American flag is defaced, with all that the flag means—yes, all that it *symbolizes*—is to ask too much of Americans.

There are symbols and there are Symbols. There are some so rooted in history and custom, and in the heroic imagination of a nation, that they transcend the merely symbolic; they become presences.

Reprinted by permission of Steve Kelley.

Many of us may not have the words to express it (which is why nations wave flags instead of computer printouts), but we know it's right to protect the flag—by law. To do nothing when that flag, that presence, is desecrated is not simply to let the violent bear it away; it is to join the mob, to aid and abet it by our silence, our permission, our unnatural law. It is to become one more accessory to the general coarsening of society, to the desensitizing of America, to the death of the symbolic.

No, this is not an argument over who loves the flag more. Patriots can disagree; American ones almost have an obligation to.

This Republic was not conceived as some kind of factory for manufacture of robots. And those on the other side of this issue have every right to resent it if somebody wants to turn this disagreement over law and the role of the symbolic in American life into some kind of loyalty test. No one political persuasion has a monopoly on the American flag. May it long wave over every kind of political rally.

But this also isn't a fight over who loves the Bill of Rights more. And those of us who favor a simple constitutional amendment to protect the flag have every reason to resent it when others try to monopolize the Bill of Rights, or confuse it with the Supreme Court's confused reading of the First Amendment where the flag is concerned.

Burning the flag is no more speech than vandalizing a cemetery, or scrawling slogans on a church or synagogue, or spray-painting a national monument—all of which are *acts* properly forbidden by the laws of a civilized country. Not to mention public decency.

Even if no flag were ever burned, or no cemetery or church ever defaced, laws against such acts would be proper, and should be constitutional. Because the law is a great teacher, and one thing it needs to teach a less-and-less-civil society is a little respect.

The great Italian—what? historian? philosopher? moralist? philosopher of history? proto-anthropologist?—Giambattista Vico spoke of a barbarism of the intellect that confuses concept with reality (speech with action?) and so loses touch with the *sensus communis*, the common-sense values of language and custom in which nations are rooted. Today's strange arguments from our best-and-brightest against protecting the national emblem are not symptomatic of any kind of treason-of-the-intellectuals, but of a different malady: an isolating intellectualism cut off from a sense of reverence, and so from the historical memory and heroic imagination that determines the fate of any nation.

"The proposed amendment [banning flag burning] could trump the First Amendment, but only at the cost of gutting its fundamental protection of free political expression."

Flag Burning Should Not Banned

Jeffrey P. Kaplan

In June 1995, the U.S. House of Representatives passed a constitutional amendment banning the burning of the American flag. In the following viewpoint, Jeffrey P. Kaplan argues against the amendment. He contends that flag burning is protected by the First Amendment because it is a form of political communication. Kaplan, who holds a law degree from the University of San Diego in California, is an associate professor of linguistics at San Diego State University.

As you read, consider the following questions:

1. What types of language and conduct does Kaplan list as being protected by the First Amendment?
2. What three components of communication does the author identify?

Jeffrey P. Kaplan, "Flag-Burning Ban: Protecting What It Symbolizes or the Symbol?" *San Diego Union-Tribune*, December 14, 1995. Reprinted by permission.

Should we amend the Constitution to let Congress ban flag desecration? An amendment to that effect has been proposed, and its supporters vow that it won't go away. Polls indicate that up to 80 percent of Americans find such an amendment desirable. But the better term may be "seductive."

The word "speech" in the First Amendment covers speech, writing, sign language, Morse code, auction gestures, etc.—any way we encode meanings in language. More importantly, the Supreme Court has applied the free speech guarantee through the years not just to language, but to conduct: picketing, sitting-in, contributing money to political candidates, displaying a red banner as a symbol of opposition to government, wearing a military uniform in a manner calculated to discredit the military, wearing a black armband to protest the Vietnam War, civil rights boycotts of merchants and displaying a U.S. flag with a peace symbol attached.

What unites all these forms of conduct is that they function as communication. In fact, what the First Amendment really guarantees is freedom of communication, according to Loyola law professor (and linguist) Peter Tiersma in a 1993 article in the *Wisconsin Law Review*.

Defining Communication

Is flag-burning communication? What is communication? First, it involves meaning. While sometimes a communicative act naturally resembles its meaning—as in pointing and beckoning—most human communication involves symbols, to which meaning attaches "conventionally." The word "road" means road, despite the fact that the sequence of sounds represented by "r," "oa," and "d" doesn't resemble a road at all.

In the same arbitrary way, a swastika represents Nazism, a black armband symbolizes mourning the dead, and a peace symbol means opposition to war. Meaningless vocalizations like "Gleeg!" aren't communicative; and conduct that doesn't encode a meaning—sleeping, eating a doughnut—generally isn't communicative either.

Flag-burning is meaningful. Ceremonial book- and effigy-burnings indicate that burning can carry the meaning of harsh condemnation. This meaning arises partly naturally: Burning is an effective way to destroy something we hate.

The meaning is partly conventional: Burning is just one of many ways to show strong revulsion (others: averting eyes, making illegal, smashing); and burning does not always operate as a symbol for condemnation (as when we burn trash). The symbolic function of burning arises only in ritual contexts.

Second, communication requires an audience. Talking to oneself isn't really communicative. The flag-burning addressed by the proposed amendment is effective, from the flag burner's perspective, only when carried out before an audience.

Third, to be communication, an instance of language must be intended by the speaker or actor to have a meaning. The monkey at the typewriter who fortuitously produces the text of *Hamlet* does not intend the words to have meaning, though they do. There is no communication because there is no intent.

Reprinted by permission of Clay Bennett.

Intentional meaningfulness is necessary also for communicative, nonverbal conduct. Placing lights in Boston's Old North Church any night but April 18, 1775, would probably not have manifested an intent to convey meaning, but that night, placing them there did, and Paul Revere understood the intended meaning.

Political flag-burners intend their act to have meaning, since the point is not to reduce fabric to ashes, but to dramatically express hatred toward what the flag symbolizes.

Actually, for communication, the essential intent is, subtly, more than just intending that words or acts have meaning. The speaker or actor must intend the audience to recognize, in the words or action, the intention to communicate.

Awaiting service in a tavern, you might clear your throat in order to get noticed. That's not communication. But if you clear your throat in an exaggerated way, it is; you intend to get the

40

bartender to recognize not only that you seek attention but also that you are making a noise in order to signal that.

Flag-burners similarly intend to communicate by having their audience recognize the intention embodied in their act, and they fail if no one recognizes what they are doing. Imagine their personal frustration if an observer compliments them for disposing of a soiled flag.

Offensive Communication

Flag-burning is communication. Because it is so striking a form of communication, with such offensive content, many Americans want to empower the state to ban it.

But since its content is quintessentially political, it receives First Amendment protection, even though—and partly because— it is so offensive. The proposed amendment could trump the First Amendment, but only at the cost of gutting its fundamental protection of free political expression.

The flag itself is a symbol. The words of the Pledge of Allegiance "with liberty and justice for all" suggest that it symbolizes, beyond the nation, ideals of liberty, including, presumably, First Amendment liberties.

Those who would change the Constitution to permit Congress to ban flag-burning must face two questions: Which is more important to defend, the symbol, or what it symbolizes? Is it rational to seek to shield the former at the cost of damaging the latter?

"*More and more professors have to censor themselves.*"

Regulations on Sexually Harassing Speech Are Excessive

Nat Hentoff

Nat Hentoff, who has been a columnist for the *Village Voice* since 1957, frequently writes in defense of free speech. In the following viewpoint, Hentoff reports that increasing numbers of college professors are being falsely accused of sexual harassment based on their speech. He contends that these cases, which are tried before college judicial boards, have had a chilling effect on speech on college campuses and have thereby damaged the education environment.

As you read, consider the following questions:

1. On what grounds does the author criticize college judicial boards?
2. According to the author, why is the case of Leroy Young important?
3. What is Cathryn Adamsky's view on sexual harassment law, as described by Hentoff?

Nat Hentoff, "'The Chill Is On,'" *Village Voice*, December 28, 1993. Reprinted with permission.

"How easy it is to take down anyone with just a flick of the pen."

—from "Political Correctness Becomes Permanent Chill,"
by Clare Kittredge, *Boston Globe*, November 14, 1993

The American Association of University Professors released a report in 1991 castigating those journalists who were making a big deal out of "political correctness." Journalists like me. Nonsense, said the AAUP. The problem is vastly exaggerated. Free inquiry is in no danger on college campuses.

I dissected that report in the *Village Voice*, but of more importance to the AAUP, there was so much rebellion from professors around the country who had been battered by political correctness that the AAUP retreated and issued a more realistic analysis. Recently, I talked with a professor who had a lot to do with generating that initial report, and he is properly embarrassed.

Indeed he is now at work on how colleges and universities can come up with free-speech alternatives to the speech codes and other products of the smothering new orthodoxy created by the various forms of political correctness. Included will be the baleful effect of college administrators' encouragement of the marginalization of minority students by self-segregation.

Marina Budhos, coordinating editor for the National Council for Research on Women, is not yet embarrassed because of her new report, but I expect she will be. Speaking for her organization, Budhos claims that the press, by focusing "on a few incidents," has created a distorted view of what's happening on campuses. She scorns the notion that there is "a new McCarthyism" in the realm of higher education.

"The p.c. debates," she blithely proclaims, "mask the challenge of making higher education more accessible to all."

But when more and more professors have to censor themselves for fear of being charged with malignant heresy, what kind of access to education is that for their students (not all of whom are p.c.)? And what happens to a professor's courage to freely inquire into his field when sitting before him in a class are multiple Madame Defarges and their male counterparts?

College Judicial Boards

Also, increasingly, professors' careers are being blighted by charges of sexual harassment from women students—charges tried before politicized judicial boards that are a mockery of due process. These college court-martials deny basic rights not only to these professors but also to students brought up on all kinds of charges.

The Student Press Law Center has begun an investigation of these disgraceful tribunals on both prestigious and not-so-prestigious campuses. Not a word from Marina Budhos on the

epidemic violations of due process on the nation's campuses—
violations that are inflicted on many of the minority students
whose greater access to higher education she wants. But what
are they learning about constitutional democracy?

As for the weapon of sexual harassment, the cases [examined
here] have nothing to do with physical harassment—touching,
feeling, groping. (The Packwood approach.) That is not protected
speech. Neither are quid pro quo cases. (Have sex with me or
you're fired. Have sex with me or you lose your promotion.)

Also not protected are certain patterns of verbal harassment—
persistent comments about how a woman looks or would be in
bed. You can't study with a clear mind while that kind of pressure is on you.

What's happening on college campuses is quite another kind
of sexual harassment. In the *Boston Globe*, Clare Kittredge has
been lucidly covering the accusations against University of New
Hampshire professor J. Donald Silva. . . .

On November 14, 1993, Kittredge reported on some of the
other cases against professors at the University of New Hampshire:

"What is ripening on state university campuses, some critics
say, is the kind of mood that fostered the Salem witch trials.
One University of New Hampshire professor says he felt the icy
fear of orthodox correct speech when his conversational campus
use of the phrase 'more bang for your buck' caused a female
student to gasp.

"'I said, "What's the matter, did you think that was a sexual
reference?"' recalled UNH English professor Tom Carnicelli.

"When the student nodded, he said he told her that 'getting
more bang for your buck' is derived from military slang about
explosives.

"'I was really shaken by that,' said the professor. 'If I hadn't
heard her gasp, she might have thought it was a sexual reference
and secretly reported me, and I might have been under a cloud.'"

Professors Under Attack

Kittredge also wrote about Leroy Young, a professor accused
of sexual harassment at Plymouth State College (which is part of
the University of New Hampshire). Critics there of the college's
handling of the charge say, according to Kittredge, that "whatever the outcome of that case, Leroy Young's teaching career
has already been seriously tainted."

Young has been asked to withdraw on paid leave. "The charges,"
says the *Globe* reporter, "remain murky." But Jim Hansen, whose
daughter was one of Leroy's students, is outraged at the charges
and has described one of them as the professor's complimenting a
female student on her new blazer. And—Clare Kittredge adds—

there are "anonymous accusations of having 'pornography'—*others call them art books*—in his office." (Emphasis added.) Professor Young teaches graphics.

Hansen angrily wrote University of New Hampshire chancellor William J. Farrell: "Apparently the Plymouth State College administration holds that *sexual harassment is entirely in the eye of the harassee, thus little can be offered as defense. This case shows how easy it is to take down anyone with the flick of a pen.*" (Emphasis added.)

Dealing with Sexism

I believe that sexist speech can lose its constitutional immunity from punishment *if* there is a persistent pattern of abusive words, gestures, or other symbols directed at specifically targeted individuals in situations from which they cannot, as a practical matter, escape; *if* fair warning has been given that the communication in question is unwelcome and inappropriate; and *if* the effect upon the victims is to interfere demonstrably with their ability to function effectively in that environment. The very same criteria should apply to hate speech based upon the target's race, religion, ethnicity, or sexual orientation.

Although legal remedies may be constitutionally permissible, and perhaps even necessary, for the narrow set of circumstances just described, they may not be the wisest or most productive course of action in dealing with the problem of sexism. They do little or nothing to cure the causes of that disease, any more than the banning of racist speech gets rid of group prejudice and hatred.

Franklyn S. Haiman, *"Speech Acts" and the First Amendment*, 1993.

As for Professor Young, Kittredge noted that "Young would only say he is a feminist deeply distressed at finding himself in a tarpit of hearsay and innuendo. 'I am not guilty of sexual harassment. I have never sexually harassed any student,' he said in a voice choked with emotion.

"'I've been in teaching for 20-something years,' Young said, 'and this is just breaking my heart. . . . I'm looking forward to a chance to clear my name, and I won't stop until I do.'"

But is it possible to ever entirely clear your name of charges of sexual harassment?

Chilling Speech

It's getting worse at the University of New Hampshire, and not only on that campus. Writes Kittredge:

"At UNH, where a 'nonsexist language policy' is reportedly

now in force, some professors say they will no longer see any students behind closed doors; others say they are terrified of anonymous accusations by immature or untutored students; one disgruntled professor said the campus mood is so chilly he may stop teaching altogether."

The phrase "chilling speech" is in common use among many of the faculty. Writes Kittredge: "Another UNH professor using 20th century blues and swing lyrics in a humanities course said he recently placed an asterisk next to a selection warning students: 'Vulgar lyrics. Listen at your own risk'—a precaution he would have considered ludicrous for college-age students 20 years ago.

"'The chill is on,' he said."

A recent report circulating among the faculty tells of a colleague in trouble because he discussed bawdy classics in class.

Not all the faculty at UNH deplore the hypersensitive learning environment. Kittredge interviewed Cathryn Adamsky, coordinator of Women's Studies at UNH. Adamsky, who has been active in the women's movement since the 1970s, said:

"As far as I'm concerned, political correctness is all right because it's being sensitive to the political aspirations of all people. I think it's shabby for people to claim they're intimidated when they're the ones with the most objective power."

But male professors Donald Silva and Leroy Young, and many more around the country, are under suspension or have been fired without due process. Where is their power?

The Adamsky argument seems to be that since there has been injustice in the past—and indeed there has been—it's okay for gender injustice to go the other way now. This is higher education as retribution.

Adamsky, for instance, went on to give more of her philosophy of education: "I can't feel terribly sorry for them [professors such as Silva], because the opportunity for women and minorities to have a voice on campus has been very limited historically."

Shoddy Charges

But Adamsky doesn't realize that what goes around comes around. Now that there are celebratory precedents on campuses to destroy the careers of white male professors on the basis of guillotine-like stereotyping, male black professors will inevitably be in the dock. Indeed, some already are—with much resultant damage to their careers.

Nor will women—even possibly Ms. Adamsky—be exempt from shoddy charges of sexual harassment. . . . Toni Blake, a graduate student and instructor at the University of Nebraska, . . . is being charged with sexual harassment by a male student because of something she said in class.

46

It is true that in many colleges, classes consist of students of varied backgrounds. Some from orthodox religious homes, and some from extremely right-wing political families. And there are students who, because of very disturbing experiences in their lives, are confused and apprehensive about sexual language and thoughts.

A teacher's remarks, analogies, and metaphors can be taken by one of those students to have created—using the current legal term—a hostile educational environment for her. Or him.

What should a professor do? Try to be sensitive, but not at the price of self-censorship.

"When a student can direct what I teach," Toni Blake told me, "my job as an educator is void."

I know of professors who are tape-recording their lectures so they'll have accurate evidence of what they said if they're brought to judgment. These professors don't get it. Accuracy is what the politically correct judges are after.

Yet . . . a *New York Times* editorial writer insists that political correctness is a cliché—that should be retired—and anyway, he says, the term is part of a right-wing conspiracy to discredit the left.

> *"The law against sexual harassment really . . . need not be another battleground between the sexes, or between censorship and the First Amendment."*

Regulations on Sexually Harassing Speech Are Not Excessive

George Rutherglen

George Rutherglen is the O.M. Vicars Professor of Law at the University of Virginia. In the following viewpoint, he argues that laws against sexual harassment in universities and in the workplace do not infringe on the right to free speech. Sexually harassing speech is not protected by the First Amendment, Rutherglen maintains, and laws designed to prevent such speech do not interfere with an individual's right to express his or her political opinions.

As you read, consider the following questions:

1. Under sexual harassment law, according to the author, what is required of a plaintiff who alleges to have been sexually harassed?
2. According to Rutherglen, on what grounds have Michael McDonald and others argued that a hostile sexual environment is constitutionally protected?
3. How does the author illustrate his argument that speech that is constitutionally protected can be regulated?

George Rutherglen, "Sexual Harassment: Ideology or Law?" Reprinted with permission from the *Harvard Journal of Law & Public Policy* 18 (Spring 1995): 487–99. Copyright 1995, Harvard Society for Law and Public Policy, Inc.

If we take the comments of Maggie Gallagher and Michael McDonald seriously, we now find ourselves in the midst of a great liberal witch hunt where the law of sexual harassment is used to enforce political correctness. I have no doubt that the law of sexual harassment could be misunderstood to serve this purpose, but in this respect, I think, it is more sinned against than sinning. Upon closer inspection, the actual law scarcely resembles the caricature that has been offered by its detractors—or occasionally, for that matter, by its supporters. The law of sexual harassment instead is surprisingly moderate, and for reasons that should have wide appeal, even if they do not satisfy those who would drastically restrict or expand its scope.

The framers of the law of sexual harassment are not the feminist, leftist liberals of conservative myth. The author of existing law is not Catharine MacKinnon, although she must be recognized as the single individual most responsible for raising the issue of sexual harassment. And neither is it the Equal Employment Opportunity Commission (EEOC), although this agency formulated the single most influential guideline on sexual harassment. Instead, the unlikely leaders of this supposed liberal witch hunt are Chief Justice William Rehnquist and Justice Sandra Day O'Connor, who, respectively, wrote the opinions in *Meritor Savings Bank v. Vinson* and *Harris v. Forklift Systems, Inc.* The standard established in these cases requires a plaintiff who alleges a hostile environment to prove that sexual advances and comments are "sufficiently severe or pervasive 'to alter the conditions of [the victim's] employment and create an abusive working environment.'" Correctly understood and applied, this standard raises few questions under the First Amendment. To the extent that it raises any problems at all, they are problems of implementation, mainly in evaluating conflicting evidence of sexual harassment. . . .

An Invalid Argument

Mr. McDonald and others have relied upon a variant of an old argument to find that a hostile sexual environment is constitutionally protected by the First Amendment. The argument is this: Forms of expression that are not obscene and that do not aid independently illegal conduct constitute protected speech under the First Amendment. Because such forms of expression—in particular, various forms of soft-core pornography and other non-obscene speech—can create a hostile sexual environment, any liability imposed on employers for engaging in or allowing such forms of expression violates the First Amendment. For all its appealing simplicity, this argument is simply invalid. It does not follow from the fact that speech is entitled to some protection under the First Amendment that it is entitled to complete protection, or, to be precise, to as much protection as political speech in a public forum.

This fallacy becomes plain in exactly the kind of case discussed by Mr. McDonald: discipline of a professor in a state university for remarks made in class. I happen to teach at a state-supported law school. Suppose that I became bored with my course in Civil Procedure and decided to devote several weeks to telling dirty jokes instead of teaching pleading and discovery. Suppose further that each of these dirty jokes had some redeeming social value, so that none were legally obscene. Nevertheless, it is clear that I could be disciplined for this lapse of professional judgment. Now suppose that instead of telling dirty jokes, I simply seized on every possible opportunity to make demeaning remarks about women, expressing the view that women had no place in the legal profession. Again, my remarks would be constitutionally protected, arguably as political speech, but in a course on Civil Procedure, they would count simply as poor teaching.

Commonsensical Law

The law on sexual harassment is clear and commonsensical. In unanimous decisions handed down in 1986 and in 1993, the Supreme Court defined sexual harassment expansively, outlawing not only so-called quid pro quo harassment—in which a boss demands sexual favors—but the "hostile work environment." As Justice Sandra Day O'Connor put it, that means a workplace "permeated with discriminatory intimidation, ridicule, and insult."

In the fall of 1993, feminists won another major victory when the Supreme Court unanimously ruled that a woman need not have a nervous breakdown in order to prove that she'd been harmed by working in such an atmosphere.

Elaine Shannon, *Vogue*, August 1994.

Nor does this argument fare any better when it is framed in terms of academic freedom rather than protected speech. The constitutional protection for academic freedom must necessarily be qualified, not absolute. Suppose that I made my remarks about the appropriate role of women in a course on employment discrimination law. Such remarks are plainly relevant to the course, but if they had the predictable effect of antagonizing all the female students in the class, these effects could be taken into account in evaluating my teaching. The point, which I will not belabor further, is that otherwise constitutionally protected speech is routinely evaluated in the academic setting without raising any claim of absolute protection under the First Amendment. Anyone who has any further doubts should merely consider the evaluations used in considering a teacher for tenure.

What holds true inside the ivory tower, at least in this one situation, also holds true outside it. Speech that receives constitutional protection may still be regulated and restricted, so long as it is not entirely prohibited. For example, certain forms of speech, such as commercial speech, receive only qualified protection. Additionally, all constitutional scholars recognize that some forms of speech, notably political speech, receive greater protection. Even if they do not agree with this principle, they recognize it as an accurate statement of existing law. As Justice John Paul Stevens wrote in a case allowing regulation of pornographic movies that were not legally obscene, "few of us would march our sons and daughters off to war to preserve the citizen's right to see 'Specified Sexual Activities' exhibited in the theaters of our choice."

Harassing Speech in the Workplace

Similarly, few of us should be concerned about the regulation of sexually harassing speech within the workplace. The supervisor's statement in *Harris*, that the plaintiff was "a dumb ass woman," does not require absolute constitutional protection. Equally undeserving of such protection is the pervasive display of soft-core pornography. The crucial question in these cases, and in the case of J. Donald Silva, a college professor accused of sexual harassment, is not the constitutional question whether the speech was immune from regulation. Undoubtedly it was not. The crucial question is whether the speech was so "severe or pervasive" as to constitute sexual harassment. An isolated remark in casual conversation or a single pin-up inside a locker door does not satisfy this definition of a sexually hostile environment, a definition that the Court formulated wholly apart from free speech concerns. The law against sexual harassment seldom raises any substantial questions under the First Amendment because it applies only to speech already found to constitute "severe or pervasive" harassment.

This practical conclusion from existing legal doctrine is obvious enough, but curiously it has been overlooked in the debates over sexual harassment. Its neglect is all the more puzzling because this conclusion reveals important structural similarities between the law of sexual harassment and the law of free speech. In both areas of law, judges evaluate individual decisions about appropriate gender roles only when necessary to secure equal opportunity for members of both sexes. Under the First Amendment, an employer is free to espouse and publicize his views about the proper role of women in society, even if the women

51

who work for him find his views offensive. Likewise, the law of sexual harassment leaves an employer free to express those views, but he cannot use them as an excuse to deny women an equal opportunity to work in his business. Contrary to what its critics fear—and some of its supporters hope—the law of sexual harassment does not take a position on the inherent desirability of different gender roles, only on their exclusivity. Gender roles cannot be used to deny women and men equal opportunities for employment. Otherwise, like the First Amendment, the law of sexual harassment leaves the question of appropriate gender roles to be resolved by the individuals themselves.

Nor does this result follow only from liberal principles of sexual equality. It also follows from general libertarian principles of limiting governmental interference with sexual conduct. All of us should be concerned about judicial activism in making nice distinctions between proper and improper sexual advances. The "young in one another's arms" is not a subject for old men—or any judge of any age.

In a diverse society like ours, in which several different gender roles are possible for anyone, and all are objectionable to someone, only the most extreme forms of expression should be excluded from the workplace. "Extreme," in this context, should have a quite specific meaning: likely to deny women equal opportunities for employment. The law against sexual harassment is not a license for judges to censor appropriate speech and manners in the workplace. Limited by the First Amendment's protection of political speech, this form of judicial regulation guarantees only equal opportunity, not proper etiquette. An employer who made general statements about his social philosophy, such as his belief that a woman's place is in the home, would not be held liable for harassment on that ground. I know of no case that has imposed liability for such a careful statement of political views. On the contrary, the standard of "severe or pervasive" harassment has been a significant barrier to finding liability based on a hostile environment. . . .

Beyond Hot Air

If we step back from overheated arguments and look at what the law against sexual harassment really is, we see that it need not be another battleground between the sexes, or between censorship and the First Amendment, or between Eros and its enemies. Despite the best efforts of its critics—and some of its supporters—the law should not be inflated into a vehicle for transforming sexual relations in our society. It is enough if it contributes to the opportunities of women in economic and public life. In just the few decades since Title VII of the 1964 Civil Rights Act first prohibited gender discrimination in employment, that change has been dramatic enough. There is no doubt that more and better changes could have been brought about, and in some instances, fewer and more effective changes. If legal reform is to be improved, however, it requires some attention to what the law is and what the facts are.

Paul Samuelson, in a memorable phrase, remarked that in disputes over methodology, Gresham's Law takes the form: "Hot air drives out cold." We would do well to apply the same observation to controversies over the law of sexual harassment.

"Art is not threatened by a cutoff of federal dollars."

Government Funding of the Arts Should Be Eliminated

L. Brent Bozell III

L. Brent Bozell III is chairman of the Media Research Center, a conservative media watchdog organization. In the following viewpoint, Bozell argues that critics are wrong to assert that cutting government funding of the arts threatens free speech or undermines America's democratic principles. He concludes that federal funding of the arts should be discontinued because the country can no longer afford such subsidies, because the private sector provides adequate support for the arts, and because controlling the arts is not the federal government's responsibility.

As you read, consider the following questions:

1. According to the author, what do Barbra Streisand and Robert Redford believe motivates efforts to cut NEA funding?
2. How have journalists characterized attempts to cut NEA funding, according to Bozell?

L. Brent Bozell III, "Circling the Arts Welfare Wagons: Panicky Defenders," *Washington Times*, March 4, 1995. Reprinted by permission of L. Brent Bozell III and Creators Syndicate.

Budget-cutters on Capitol Hill are eyeing the Corporation for Public Broadcasting and the National Endowment for the Arts. . . . It's panic time for these agencies' defenders in the entertainment media, who are becoming increasingly vocal, promoting a dubious idea of artistic freedom: the "right" to taxpayer money. They label anyone disagreeing with them as not just wrong but barbaric, even dictatorial.

Singer/actress/director/gadfly Barbra Streisand extolled federal arts funding and insinuated darkly about those who oppose it in a Feb. 3, 1995, speech at Harvard's Kennedy School of Government. "Maybe it's not about balancing the budget," Miss Streisand suggested. "Maybe it's about shutting the minds and mouths of artists who might have something thought provoking to say."

The diva went on: "To deny artists . . . free expression and free thought—or, worse, to force us to conform to some rigid notion of 'mainstream American values'—is to weaken the very foundation of our democracy."

La-La Land Conspiracy Theory

Why does anyone take this lady seriously? To suggest this debate has nothing to do with balancing the budget but is instead a plot by conservatives to undermine democracy is the stuff of La-La Land conspiracy theories. The NEA's $165 million budget represents less than 2 percent of the $9 billion contributed to the arts every year through the private sector, a figure that represents the greatest private philanthropic investment in the arts in the history of man. Even Harvard can see that art is not threatened by a cutoff of federal dollars.

Miss Streisand is not alone. Her "The Way We Were" co-star, Robert Redford, also believes a dastardly cabal is at work, telling USA Today on Jan. 24, 1995, that: "It's pretty clear we're always going to be fighting this battle. There's always going to be some conservative group that is threatened by freedom, by free ideas and by free expression in general."

Actor Christopher ("Superman") Reeve is somewhat more pragmatic. An outspoken liberal, he would like expanded NEA funding but knows that isn't realistic. Mr. Reeve told a Senate subcommittee on Feb. 23, 1995, that he favors privatizing the NEA over several years via a matching-funds process. On the other hand, Mr. Reeve continues to promote, as he did on John McLaughlin's "One on One" show Feb. 25 and 26, the canard that the Robert Mapplethorpe and Andres Serrano NEA grants were accidents, that the agency would never knowingly countenance such filth. Not so, corrected his "One on One" adversary, former National Endowment for the Humanities chief Lynne Cheney: the NEA *knew precisely* what it was doing.

Some journalists covering entertainment and the arts are

equally hyperbolic in their defense of cultural subsidies. . . .
John Leonard, TV critic for CBS's "Sunday Morning," compared
budget-conscious Republicans to murderous dictators on the
Jan. 8, 1995, broadcast: "From the pronunciamentos out of
Washington, you'd think the new Congress were a slash-and-
burn Khmer Rouge, determined to rid Phnom Penh of every
member of the Corporation for Public Broadcasting, every
painter who ever got a dime out of the National Endowment for
the Arts . . . and other inconvenient co-dependents."

"IT'S CALLED 'SELF-PORTRAIT OF AN ARTIST WHO JUST GOT $75,000
FROM THE NATIONAL ENDOWMENT FOR THE ARTS'!"

Likewise, *Washington Post* TV critic Tom Shales and his Jan.
25, 1995, review of Bill Clinton's State of the Union speech. Mr.
Clinton spoke for what seemed like a day and a half, but, Mr.
Shales griped, he still didn't find time to plug welfare for mil-
lionaire Muppets: "Too bad he didn't say a word or two on behalf of public broadcasting, currently under attack by a crowd
of power-drunk crackpots in Congress who want to exterminate
it. Kermit the Frog will wind up in the kitchen of a French
restaurant if they get their way."
    While Mr. Shales saw frog a la carte, *Los Angeles Times* arts
critic Christopher Knight, on Jan. 8, 1995, saw a different plot—
this one against diversity: "[Republicans] want the NEA gone be-

cause of its record of success. A chief accomplishment of public arts support has been that the American cultural landscape today is far more diverse than it ever was before the 1965 birth of the National Endowment for the Arts, when the private funding so dear to [Newt] Gingrich was art's sole engine."

Defenders of artistic welfare are clearly running out of gas. They cannot defend the economics of federal subsidies (the country can no longer afford it). They cannot defend the value of these multi-billion-dollar bureaucracies (the arts and cultural/educational programming is flourishing through the private sector). And they don't dare raise the most basic question: Since when was it the role of the federal government to control the arts?

"Public support for the arts is a down payment on our future."

Government Funding of the Arts Should Continue

Hillary Rodham Clinton

Hillary Rodham Clinton is honorary chairwoman of the President's Committee on the Arts and Humanities. In the following viewpoint, she argues that proposals to restrict funding of the National Endowment for the Arts (NEA) are misguided. Not only would such budget cuts hurt America's cultural institutions, Clinton maintains, but they would undermine the nation's democratic foundations by depriving citizens of exposure to the heritage of Western civilization.

As you read, consider the following questions:

1. How has the NEA helped transform whole communities, according to Clinton?
2. According to the author, what effect do the arts have on American society?

Hillary Rodham Clinton, "Arts for Our Sake," *New York Times*, June 21, 1995.

This is an ominous time for those of us who care deeply about the arts in America. A misguided, misinformed effort to eliminate public support for the arts not only threatens irrevocable damage to our cultural institutions but also to our sense of ourselves and what we stand for as a people.

One of the great successes of the arts in America is that they are not the preserve of any "cultural elite." Through museums, libraries, schools, dance companies and concerts, the arts are truly part of the public domain, accessible to all and capable of encouraging every person's artistic expression and sensibility.

The National Endowment for the Arts, in partnership with individuals, corporations, foundations and other patrons of the arts, has helped transform whole communities by bringing the arts and artists to millions who otherwise might never have had the opportunity to explore firsthand our shared artistic heritage.

The President has shown that we can balance the budget without undermining our commitment to the arts. The N.E.A. budget accounts for less than 0.02 percent of the Federal budget. Eliminating this small but vital agency would have grave consequences for local economies. Federal support for the arts helps attract tourists, stimulate business, expand the tax base and improve the quality of life—a huge return on a small investment.

Despite a 30-year bipartisan commitment to the arts, there are those who argue that public support is a luxury we can no longer afford. They mistakenly suggest that the arts are enjoyed only by a small, wealthy minority. But if public support for the arts disappears, those most affected will not be the richest Americans but the millions of citizens who rely on the N.E.A. to bring the arts to their local schools and communities.

The Artistic Imagination Is Critical

I find it ironic that those who talk the loudest about America's loss of civility, character and values (particularly those arising from Western civilization) are often the first to recommend obliterating the agencies responsible for promoting arts programs that make Sophocles, Shakespeare, Mozart and O'Keeffe available to our children.

They fail to appreciate what every generation of Americans has intuitively known—that the artistic imagination is critical to our civilization and our democracy. They forget the prescient words of John Adams: "I must study politics and war that my sons may have liberty to study mathematics and philosophy. My sons ought to study mathematics and philosophy . . . in order to give their children a right to study painting, poetry, music."

The power of the arts is not simply to provide pleasant esthetics but to help move us forward as a democracy. Human expression, as conveyed through the arts, enables us to understand better the complexities of life and gives us a bridge to the world preceding and surrounding us. Most important, exposure to our cultural traditions enriches the lives of our children.

Part of the National Economy

State governments, private businesses and foundations—organizations which usually do not have art review committees of their own—are often more willing to support art institutions and projects if the recipient has been given an NEA grant. The grant is seen as a "seal of approval" that attests to the quality of the recipient.

By generating an estimated $37 billion in economic activity each year, the not-for-profit arts sector serves an integral part of the national economy and supports over a million jobs. Many of those jobs would be lost if NEA-supported institutions were forced to cut back on employment and other resources.

Issues and Controversies on File, November 3, 1995.

Too often, we see children who, instead of discovering the joys of painting, music, sculpting or writing, express themselves through acts of frustration and even violence. The arts offer an alternative to the more disturbing elements of our popular culture, and a safe haven that allows children to explore their creative potential, transporting them beyond the bounds of their difficult circumstances. Their exposure to the roots and diverse richness of human civilization will enhance their understanding of their own heritage and the world in which they live.

Clearly our nation faces difficult choices. But as the rhetoric heats up over the role of government in our society, I hope we will remember that public support for the arts is a down payment on our future. It is an investment in the values we claim to honor and in the cultural traditions in which democracy has flourished for 218 years. Now is no time to turn our backs on that legacy or its promise.

Periodical Bibliography

The following articles have been selected to supplement the diverse views presented in this chapter. Addresses are provided for periodicals not indexed in the *Readers' Guide to Periodical Literature*, the *Alternative Press Index*, the *Social Sciences Index*, or the *Index to Legal Periodicals and Books*.

Larry Alexander	"Free Speech and Speaker's Intent," *Constitutional Commentary*, Spring 1995.
Molefi Kete Asante	"Unraveling the Edges of Free Speech," *National Forum*, Spring 1995. Available from PO Box 16000, Baton Rouge, LA 70893-1410.
Winton M. Blount	"Don't Privatize Art," *New York Times*, March 27, 1995.
Stanley C. Brubaker	"In Praise of Censorship," *Public Interest*, Winter 1994.
Samuel Francis	"What's at Issue Is Not Really 'Free Speech,'" *Conservative Chronicle*, May 8, 1996. Available from PO Box 29, Hampton, IA 50441-0029.
Steven Hill	"Speech May Be Free, but It Sure Isn't Cheap," *Humanist*, May/June 1994.
Robert Hughes	"The Case for Elitist Do-Gooders," *New Yorker*, May 27, 1996.
Paul K. McMasters	"Teach Kids the Value of Free Expression," *American Journalism Review*, January/ February 1994. Available from 8701 Adelphi Rd., Adelphi, MD 20783-1716.
Annabel Patterson	"More Speech on Free Speech," *Modern Language Quarterly*, March 1993. Available from 4045 Brooklyn Ave. NE, Seattle, WA 98105.
Steven D. Smith	"Radically Subversive Speech and the Authority of Law," *Michigan Law Review*, November 1995.
Mark Tushnet	"New Meaning for the First Amendment: Free Speech May Be Seen as a Tool for Protecting Those in Power," *ABA Journal*, November 1995.
Gene Edward Veith	"The National Endowment for the Arts: Liberator or Warden? *Current*, November 1995.

Is Censorship Occurring in Schools and Libraries?

CENSORSHIP

Chapter Preface

In 1988 the Supreme Court ruled in *Hazelwood School District v. Kuhlmeier* that public school officials have the right to censor student publications that are not public forums. The decision involved a high school principal who wished to prevent the identity of an unwed mother, who was a student at the school, from being published in the school newspaper.

Critics view the *Hazelwood* decision as a threat to free speech. In response to the ruling, many have called on state legislatures to pass laws giving increased powers to high school journalists. One proponent of such legislation, Robert J. Shoop, a professor of educational administration at Kansas State University, contends that states must now act to ensure that student journalists "have the same rights and responsibilities as any other journalist."

Others, however, do not consider the *Hazelwood* decision to be a violation of free speech rights. J. Michael Aytes, the assistant superintendent of the Unified School District in Concordia, Kansas, argues that the *Hazelwood* decision merely makes the high school principal the equivalent of an editor in chief. High school journalists, he maintains, should be no more free to publish whatever they want than are professional journalists, whose work is overseen by editors. Under *Hazelwood*, he writes, school newspapers will "remain part of the curriculum," and there is no "reason for them to become open forums for students to criticize other students, faculty, or programs."

Whether the work of student journalists should be subject to censorship is among the issues considered in the following chapter on censorship in schools and libraries. In addition, commentators debate whether books are being banned from the schools, whether educational materials are being censored due to their ideological content, and whether speech codes on college campuses are justified as a means of preventing harassment of minorities and women. Central to all these debates is the belief that decisions affecting the school environment and the content of education curriculums will influence the beliefs and attitudes of the young.

"Library officials say the wave of book bannings and restrictions has never been higher."

Books Are Being Banned

Michael Granberry

In the following viewpoint, Michael Granberry argues that books are increasingly being banned from schools and libraries by both liberals and conservatives. According to Granberry, conservatives wishing to ban books that are sexually explicit have now been joined by liberals attempting to exclude books characterized by ageism, sexism, and racism. Granberry is a staff writer for the *Los Angeles Times*.

As you read, consider the following questions:

1. According to Granberry, why did Kathy McNamara agree to remove Maya Angelou's *I Know Why the Caged Bird Sings* from her school's reading list?
2. Why are those who support censorship often more successful than those who oppose censorship, according to the author?
3. What new trend, reported by Granberry, did the People For the American Way survey detect in 1991–1992?

Through no desire of her own, Kathy McNamara came to be known as "the book banner from Banning." Colleagues kidded her about it, but most of the time, she bristled at the joke. It just wasn't funny. Censorship and the death of a friend never are.

Against her better judgment, McNamara, the principal at Susan B. Coombs Middle School, had removed Maya Angelou's autobiography, *I Know Why the Caged Bird Sings*, from a required reading list.

Parents of students in the eighth-grade class where the book was introduced by teacher Deborah Bennett became so incensed over sexual references in Angelou's stirring story of heartache and triumph that they demanded the book be banned.

McNamara still seethes at the memory of how she grudgingly complied—largely because she feared that stress brought on by the controversy was causing Bennett's fragile health to worsen. She believes that the nastiness of the affair hastened her friend's death. Within months of being confronted by outraged parents, Bennett, 44, died of lung and breast cancer.

"I swore that after that last piece of dirt was thrown on her casket, I would never again let happen to another teacher what happened to Deborah," McNamara said. "Because of those parents, she went through hell."

Teachers and administrators in Banning, California, are hardly alone in facing the wrath of an increasingly vocal breed of activist parent who objects to the books children are exposed to in classrooms and school libraries. And the war on books is extending well beyond the realms of schools.

Library officials say the wave of book bannings and restrictions has never been higher and that books are merely the latest in a long line of targets that include controversial artworks funded with public money and music with provocative lyrics.

People for the American Way, a political action group formed by television producer Norman Lear (*All in the Family*), monitors book bannings from its Santa Monica headquarters. Spokesman Michael Hudson said the statistics are troubling and getting worse.

Reports of censorship in public schools increased 50% in 1992, Hudson said, noting that the number of incidents was the highest since the group began its annual survey in 1982.

Whether the issue is a photograph by the late Robert Mapplethorpe, a song called "Cop Killer" or Madonna's picture book called, simply, *Sex*, critics and wanna-be censors have ceased to be shy. Some targets are as seemingly innocent as readers for first-graders.

"They always say the same thing," McNamara said. "'I don't want my tax dollars paying for that trash.' Well, the rest of us had better wake up and realize that we have tax dollars, too.

Isn't a free country worth paying for?"

Many fear that when it comes to books, librarians and school officials often do not muster the same backbone as record executives or the heads of art institutions. The result seems to be that censors often succeed in their efforts to yank a book from a shelf.

"Problem No. 1 is that librarians and school officials aren't pulling down the same salary as the head of General Motors," said Judith F. Krug, director of the Office of Intellectual Freedom for the American Library Assn. "Problem No. 2 is that people who find themselves against the wall often perceive the fight in terms of security. And any time you pit security against freedom, security wins hands down."

The storm in Banning arose after a boy in Bennett's class showed his mother passages from Angelou's book regarding child molestation and rape. His mother, a member of a fundamentalist religious sect in rural Cabazon, showed another parent, who showed another and so forth.

Before long, Bennett and McNamara were at the center of a full-blown debate over books and the 1st Amendment. In the end, McNamara, who preferred to continue the fight, gave in, fearing a downturn in Bennett's condition.

For Angelou, the writer who composed an inauguration poem for President Clinton, the incident was just the latest in many similar cases. Her first and most popular work has been banned in classrooms and libraries throughout the country.

In Raleigh, N.C.; Bremerton, Wash.; Lafayette, La.; and Strong, Me., the complaint was much the same. The book, critics say, contains "explicit passages" and has no place in a school curriculum. The story is based on a sexual assault perpetrated against Angelou as a child, which rendered her mute for almost a decade.

"If you read parts of it out of context, it can cause great concern," said Banning's acting school superintendent, Larry Phelps. "We don't want to have any material that's offensive to people. So we held it out."

Offensive Material

Material that's offensive to people seems to be the common refrain heard from officials explaining why they restricted access to books, ranging from classics by John Steinbeck, William Faulkner and Ernest Hemingway to Dr. Seuss and even the Bible.

The American Library Assn. recorded more than 653 "incidents of attempted censorship" in 1992, but only 15% of such efforts ever "see the light of day, meaning they're reported to us or they're covered by the media," Krug said.

Krug's office recorded a 28% increase in attempted censorship between 1991 and 1992. She expects 1993 statistics to be higher, with most complaints coming from fundamentalist religious groups.

But book banning is hardly the province of right-wing extremists. Never before have groups as dissimilar as the National Assn. for the Advancement of Colored People and the Rev. Pat Robertson's Christian Coalition lobbied so fiercely for changes to school curricula or the membership of library boards, or tried so aggressively to make outlaws out of books.

The practice is as old as words on paper. The American Library Assn. has compiled a list of books banned from 387 B.C. to the present and notes the following objections: J.D. Salinger's *Catcher in the Rye* (excess vulgar language), Mark Twain's *The Adventures of Huckleberry Finn* (racist), Charles Dickens' *Oliver Twist* (full of religious bias), Faulkner's *As I Lay Dying* (offensive and obscene passages referring to abortion) and Steinbeck's *The Grapes of Wrath* (full of sacrilege).

Where's Waldo?

Recent entries include one book in the popular *Where's Waldo?* series and even *Snow White*, which can be read in Jacksonville, Fla., public schools only with parental permission. The school superintendent agreed with a committee of parents and teachers that the classic fairy tale is "violent."

"If *Snow White* can be restricted, nothing is beyond reach," said Robert O'Neil of the Thomas Jefferson Center for Protection of Free Expression at the University of Virginia.

Where's Waldo? was banned from a Long Island school library because hidden among the hundreds of tiny figures crammed onto the "beach page" is a woman with a breast partially exposed. The breast is about the size of the lead tip of a pencil.

And in Erie, Pa., the mother of a ninth-grader protested after teachers used black felt-tip markers to delete passages about apes' mating habits from naturalist Dian Fossey's book *Gorillas in the Mist*. The school's principal said he permitted teachers to black out the passages, anticipating parents' concerns.

The reasons for banning books often defy belief. The Alabama State Textbook Committee once called for the rejection of *The Diary of Anne Frank*, a young girl's story of the horror of the Holocaust, because, in its words, "it is a real downer."

But there are some success stories when it comes to warding off would-be censors. In Cumberland County, N.C., fundamentalist groups demanded that two books about homosexual lifestyles be ousted from the shelves of the local library. Despite threats to defeat a library's bond measure, the head librarian stood his ground—and the measure passed.

In Colorado Springs, Colo., after the head of the library canceled the order for Madonna's *Sex* book, voters defeated his library bond measure. . . .

Just about everywhere, the figures of such incidents are climbing.

In the People for the American Way's survey of attempted book censorship in schools for 1991–1992, the Midwest region recorded the highest number—119 cases. The Northeast had the fewest of any region, 59. Florida, with 34 incidents, reported more than any other state. California and Texas were next with 27 each.

But 1991–92 also produced what Hudson called a "new and far more disturbing trend": almost an equal number of challenges to books in libraries, which before have often eluded the censors' grasps.

Library Bill of Rights

The American Library Association (ALA) affirms that all libraries are forums for information and ideas, and that the following basic policies should guide their services.

1. Books and other library resources should be provided for the interest, information, and enlightenment of all people of the community the library serves. Materials should not be excluded because of the origin, background, or views of those contributing to their creation.

2. Libraries should provide materials and information presenting all points of view on current and historical issues. Materials should not be proscribed or removed because of partisan or doctrinal disapproval.

3. Libraries should challenge censorship in the fulfillment of their responsibility to provide information and enlightenment.

Adopted June 18, 1948. Amended February 2, 1961, June 27, 1967, and January 23, 1980, by the ALA Council.

"We're talking books no one was made to read," he said. "Textbooks usually are required reading. We think it's bad and getting worse, and anyone who cares about democracy ought to wake up and do something about it."

But caring about democracy and doing something about it is precisely their intent, say the groups trying to control the content of public education and stem the tide of popular culture, much of which they find offensive.

"There is a place for censorship . . . for security reasons, or because something is inappropriate," said Robert Simonds of the

National Assn. of Christian Educators, based in Santa Ana.

"There was a time when censorship was used to protect the public good," said John Whitehead, president of the Rutherford Institute, a Christian legal foundation. "Today, certain groups are using (the charge of censorship) as a way to beat back decent people who want to see some sort of moral standards in the classroom.". . .

Although liberal groups are becoming increasingly vocal, many cite the religious right and three groups with California ties—James Dobson's Focus on the Family, which began in Pomona but is now stationed in Colorado; the Rev. Louis P. Sheldon's Traditional Values Coalition, based in Anaheim; and Simonds' Christian education movement—for waging a war on books.

The three organizations gained national attention by opposing the "Impressions Series," reading books that were challenged in schools nationwide—but particularly in California—in 1991.

A nationwide preemptive effort is being waged against two books that conservative groups say promote homosexual lifestyles and are inappropriate for public schools.

Heather Has Two Mommies and *Daddy's Roommate* feature illustrations of gay couples and are listed among hundreds of books on a suggested multicultural bibliography for New York City public schoolteachers. So far, no teacher has used the books, but that did not stop the issue of restricting classroom discussion of homosexuality from becoming a factor in 1993's hotly contested New York school board elections.

Sheldon said that in his eyes *Heather Has Two Mommies* and *Daddy's Roommate* are to "public education what gays in the military will be to Mr. Clinton. They bring God-fearing people together in a noble crusade."

Paul L. Hetrick, spokesman for Focus on the Family, said many parents have a feeling of "being utterly fed up with the mess in our public schools." Books, he said, are "just one of the tools" in an ongoing "civil war."

The growth of fundamentalist challenges to books and curricula are "rooted in a tug of war for the mind of the child—the child in America," Hetrick said, a view many seem eager to endorse.

A radical change occurred about 15 years ago when complaints took on an added texture: the *isms. Ageism, sexism, racism.* Those concerns were voiced largely by liberals, who began to question some classics, including *The Adventures of Huckleberry Finn,* as being out of step with contemporary mores. The pendulum began to swing back during the early years of Ronald Reagan's presidency. Almost immediately after 1980, the American Library Assn. recorded a fivefold increase in demands for censorship.

"False charges of banning or censorship are so common that they are seldom challenged for evidence."

Books Are Not Being Banned

Thomas Sowell

Thomas Sowell, an economist and senior fellow at the Hoover Institution, is a nationally syndicated columnist. In the following viewpoint, he maintains that charges of book banning and censorship in schools and libraries are false. He contends that school and library officials must make judgments about which books to purchase, and their decision not to buy a particular book does not constitute banning or censorship.

As you read, consider the following questions:

1. How are the terms "banned" and "censorship" being misused, in the author's opinion?
2. According to Sowell, what types of books have been declared "banned"?
3. What role should parents play in selecting books for schools, according to the author?

Thomas Sowell, "Hogwash Is Happening," *Washington Times*, October 3, 1994. Reprinted by permission of Thomas Sowell and Creators Syndicate.

Book Banning is Happening Now!! That is what the sign said in the midst of a big display in the bookstore window. As it turned out, book banning was not happening. Hogwash was happening.

The books in the display were not banned. You can get them at bookstores from sea to shining sea. The government itself buys some of them. Many of these books are circulating in the tens of thousands, and some in the millions.

A poster in the display proclaimed [the week of October 3, 1994] to be "Banned Books Week." The kind of shameless propaganda that has become commonplace in false charges of "censorship" or "book banning" has apparently now been institutionalized with a week of its own.

False Charges

Someone called the 1930s a "low, dishonest decade." The 1990s are a serious competitor for that title. False charges of banning or censorship are so common that they are seldom challenged for evidence or even for a definition.

To call a book "banned" because someone decided that it was unsuitable for their particular students or clientele would be to make at least 99 percent of all books "banned." Few individuals or institutions can afford to buy even 1 percent of the vast number of books that are published annually. They must exercise judgment and that judgment is necessarily in the negative most of the time.

If we are not going to call every book that is not purchased by an institution "banned," then how will we define this nebulous but emotional word?

Usually some school or library officials decide to buy a particular book and then some parents or others object that it is either unsuitable for children or unsuitable in general, for any of a number of reasons. Then the cry of "censorship" goes up, even if the book is still being sold openly all over town.

If the criterion of censorship is that the objection comes from the general public, rather than from people who run schools and libraries, then that is saying the parents and taxpayers have no right to a say about what is done with their own children or their own money.

This is a pretty raw assertion of pre-emptive superiority—and while many of the self-anointed may think this way, few are bold enough to come right out and say it. Fraudulent words like "censorship" and "banned" enable them to avoid saying it.

Some of the books shown seemed pretty innocuous to me—but there is no more reason why my opinion should prevail than the opinion of someone else, especially when that someone else is a parent or taxpayer. However, other books in the display were pure propaganda for avant-garde notions that are being foisted onto vulnerable and unsuspecting children in the name of "education."

Parental Rights

Parents have not only a right but a duty to object when their children are being used as objects for other people's ideological crusades, especially when brainwashing replaces education in the public schools. Let the ideologues argue their ideas openly with adults in the marketplace of ideas, not take cowardly advantage of children behind their parents' backs.

Reprinted by permission of Chuck Asay and Creators Syndicate.

There is no point arguing about whether this book or that book should or should not have been taken off the shelves. There would not be an issue in the first place if different people did not have different opinions on that point. The question is why some people's opinions are called "censorship" and other people's opinions are not.

Elite Intelligentsia

No one calls it censorship when the old McGuffey's Readers are no longer purchased by the public schools (though they are still available and are actually being used in some private schools). No one calls it censorship if the collected works of Rush Limbaugh are not put into libraries and schools in every

72

town, hamlet and middlesex village.

It is only when the books approved by the elite intelligentsia are objected to by others that it is called censorship. Apparently we are not to talk back to our betters.

All this is just one more skirmish in the cultural wars of our time. In war, someone pointed out long ago, truth is the first casualty. Those who are spreading hysteria about book banning and censorship know that they are in a war, but too many of those who thoughtlessly repeat their rhetoric do not.

It is not enough to see through fraudulent rhetoric in a particular case if you continue to listen gullibly to those who have used such rhetoric to muddy the waters.

There should have been a sign in that bookstore window saying "Hogwash is happening." That's what really rates two exclamation points—and perhaps a National Hogwash Week.

"Many individuals who seek to censor educational materials and programs view public education . . . as a vehicle for ensuring ideological conformity."

The Right Is Censoring Educational Materials

Barbara Spindel and Deanna Duby

Barbara Spindel is supervising researcher for *Attacks on the Freedom to Learn*, an annual report on censorship in public schools published by People For the American Way, an anticensorship organization created by television producer Norman Lear. Deanna Duby is director of education policy for People For the American Way. In the following viewpoint, Spindel and Duby contend that attempts at censorship by the religious right in the public schools are increasing. They describe efforts to remove and restrict classroom and library materials, to censor student newspapers and plays, and to influence various school reform measures.

As you read, consider the following questions:

1. What has been the traditionally accepted view of education, according to Spindel and Duby?
2. What school reforms do the authors say have been challenged by the religious right?
3. In what ways are clashes over school prayer similar to debates over the censorship of educational materials, according to the authors?

Barbara Spindel and Deanna Duby, "Attacks on the Freedom to Learn: People for the American Way's Report on School Censorship," 1994. Reprinted by permission of People for the American Way, Washington, D.C.

Each year since 1982, People For the American Way has published a report on challenges to educational materials and programs in the public schools, *Attacks on the Freedom to Learn*. The successive editions of the report have documented a steady rise in censorship activity that reflects an ongoing struggle to redefine education in America. The findings of 1994's *Attacks on the Freedom to Learn* demonstrate that the censorship strategy continues to play a central role in the larger effort to undermine public education. The losers in the battles this effort engenders are three: parents, whose children are denied access to ideas and materials because of the ideological and sectarian controversies being generated; teachers, who, increasingly subjected to intimidation and harassment, second-guess themselves and cleanse their classrooms of anything that might be considered controversial; and most important, the schoolchildren themselves, whose access to quality education is invariably diminished by these ideological and sectarian demands. Students are being denied the resources to develop the critical thinking skills necessary to participate and to succeed in an increasingly complex society.

It is well within parents' rights to request an alternative assignment or "opt out" for their child when they find material objectionable. School officials respond positively to such requests when they are reasonable. Requests to remove or restrict materials for all students, however—such as *Attacks on the Freedom to Learn* documents—go beyond parental involvement to an infringement on other parents' rights.

In the main, the conflicts taking shape in the public schools today mirror larger societal conflicts. Abortion, gay and lesbian rights, television violence, and funding for the arts are all issues that have lately been played out in the courts, in the media, and at the ballot box. The concerns to which these conflicts speak are some of the most elemental in this nation's history: the scope of free expression, the place of religion in public life, and the extent to which American culture should foster—or at least acknowledge—diversity. The vital role the public schools will play in determining the future direction of these debates makes them a central target.

The Role of Public Schools

To date, the generally accepted view of education has been that young people should be challenged intellectually in school, that they should be taught to think critically, to solve problems, and to use their judgment and imagination. Concomitant to this is the belief that as these skills are developed, a respect for the opinions of others should also be fostered.

Many individuals who seek to censor educational materials

and programs view public education quite differently—they see it as a vehicle for ensuring ideological conformity. This perspective favors a sectarian and reactionary schooling over one that is based on imagination, critical thinking, and recognition of pluralism. Its proponents want students to be "protected" from books and theories that may challenge a particular set of beliefs and assumptions. In short, they believe that children should be told what to think rather than how to think.

As People For the American Way's report illustrates, objectors—who often are connected to or inspired by one or more religious right political groups—are casting a wider net than ever before in their efforts to redefine public education. While censorship has, over the years, proven to be an effective strategy toward this end, more and more objectors are exploring additional means of accomplishing their goals. Research is turning up increasing numbers of incidents that, while not outright censorship, share the aim of imposing a measure of religious or political orthodoxy on the classroom—incidents such as the creation of a policy requiring teachers to list all "profane words" that appear in required reading materials, and campaigns to inject organized school prayer into the classroom.

The Scope of Challenges

The battle to define American education is comprehensive and multifaceted. People For the American Way researchers uncovered 462 challenges to educational materials or programs in the 1993–94 school year—375 cases of attempted censorship and 87 broad-based challenges to public education. Efforts to undermine the public schools are taking place in every region of the country, in cities, suburbs, and rural areas. *Attacks on the Freedom to Learn* documents challenges in forty-six states and the District of Columbia. For the second year in a row, California had the most incidents—forty-three. Texas followed, with thirty-two challenges; Florida was third, with twenty-two.

No educational materials were safe from controversy in 1993–94. Attempts were made to censor literature anthologies, biology textbooks, novels, and films used in the classroom; books and magazines available in libraries; material on optional, supplemental, and summer reading lists; school newspapers and literary magazines; self-esteem curricula; student-performed plays; and health and sexuality education curricula. And would-be censors met with remarkable success: in 42 percent of the incidents, books and other materials were removed or restricted.

In addition, challengers at the state and local levels took aim at school reform initiatives, assessment tests, graduation service requirements, and optional counseling services. Many of these groups pressed for school prayer; school choice vouchers, designed to divert public school monies to private education; and fear-based, abstinence-only sexuality education programs.

Direct Challenges to Students

Challenges to school newspapers and the students who staff them are on the rise, with objectors attempting to prevent them from covering controversial issues and school officials frequently trying to soften their criticisms of schools or school policies. School officials have based their authority largely on the Supreme Court's 1988 decision *Hazelwood v. Kuhlmeier*, which permitted a high school principal to ban articles on divorce and teenage pregnancy from the student newspaper. Five states—California, Colorado, Iowa, Kansas, and Massachusetts—have passed student freedom of expression bills, giving students broader rights than the *Hazelwood* decision allowed them. But some school officials have interpreted *Hazelwood* as granting them broad, even unchecked, authority. In some cases, student journalists who have balked at the censorship of the school-sanctioned newspapers have started their own "underground" newspapers, only to find those censored, as well.

Challenges to student theatrical productions met with an alarming measure of success in 1993–94. Objectors challenged seven student productions and succeeded in having three canceled (a student lip sync show, *Peter Pan*, and *Bats in the Belfry*) and one edited (*The Robber Bridegroom*). Challenges to productions of *Annie Get Your Gun*, *Damn Yankees*, and *Agatha Christie Made Me Do It* were unsuccessful.

Corollaries and "Alternatives" to Censorship

An alarming new trend emerged in 1992–93: across the country, educators were harassed and in some cases terminated in the wake of challenges to educational materials. In 1993–94, that trend escalated. In more and more cases, activists requesting the removal of materials added a second demand: remove the teacher, as well. For the most part, school officials and school boards stood by their staffs. In some instances, however, teachers became convenient scapegoats and were sacrificed in the face of potent pressure tactics. For example, in Mifflinburg, Pennsylvania, an anonymous complaint calling the claymation film *The Amazing Mr. Bickford* "pornographic" ultimately led to a high school English teacher's suspension without pay.

Another disturbing trend that has taken shape over the last few years involves responding to complaints about library materials by reclassifying books into different sections of the collection—to professional shelves, reserved sections, or otherwise less accessible areas. Often, the books are transferred to sections that are obscure, or less likely to be freely accessed by students.

In Laurens, South Carolina, for instance, following complaints that the book *Scary Stories to Tell in the Dark* has a "devil's theme," the title was removed from the general collection of an elementary school library and placed on a reserve shelf for teachers only. Such reclassifications signal a reluctance on the part of the schools to take a strong and vocal stand against censorship. Often, this reluctance is the result of increased pressure tactics.

Reprinted by permission of Don Addis.

The number of broad-based challenges, in which organizations or individuals applied ideological or sectarian-based pressure on the public schools without necessarily calling for the removal of specific curricular materials, roughly doubled in 1993–94, to eighty-seven. Also remarkable—and, indeed, unprecedented—is the range of materials and activities that came under scrutiny: among other activities, groups mounted campaigns against school reform, attacked state assessment tests, and helped lead an energized school prayer movement.

The Attack on School Reform

Most religious right political groups continue to challenge a wide array of educational reforms, including Goals 2000 and outcome-based education. Redesigning education around high

78

standards for student performance is at the heart of school reform, and it has been endorsed by such prominent groups as the Business Roundtable, the National Governors' Association, and the Education Commission of the States. However, outcome-based education has encountered organized and bitter opposition from a number of state and national political organizations. Activists representing these groups travel across the country as part of an intense campaign to thwart adoption of this school reform. In doing so, they use an array of vague charges and distortions while advancing a series of conspiracy theories.

The battle over outcome-based education has expanded to include federal legislation establishing the Goals 2000 program, which sets national voluntary standards and encourages local districts to involve parents and the community, including businesses, in the development of standards for local schools. Religious right political leaders have widely mischaracterized Goals 2000, omitting important information and exploiting parents' anxieties about their children's future.

Religious right political groups have used the hot-button phrase "outcome-based education" as an organizing and fund-raising tool in their broader campaign to take control of America's public schools. They have been so successful that the debate on outcome-based education has yet to focus on outcome-based education; it has instead focused on opponents' erroneous descriptions of outcome-based education. The facts have been lost in the rhetoric.

Statewide Testing

Another area of broad-based challenges involves organized efforts to scuttle California's new statewide testing system. After the Traditional Values Coalition, a California-based religious right political group, complained that Alice Walker's short story "Roselily" was "antireligious," state education officials removed the story from a pool of literature available for use in the 1994 California Learning Assessment System (CLAS), a statewide achievement examination to be administered to tenth graders. Also pulled, in a separate decision by the state board of education, were Walker's "Am I Blue?," which challengers had labeled "anti-meat-eating," and an excerpt from Annie Dillard's *An American Childhood*, for a depiction of a snowball fight challengers saw as "violent."

Controversy over the stories, which were ultimately reinstated, turned out to be only the first step in a well-organized campaign against the test—a campaign that employed the rhetoric and strategies used to cripple other education reform initiatives. Although the test was upheld in court, a number of districts voted not to administer CLAS because of the controversy.

With the legal and organizing assistance of prominent religious right groups, the school prayer movement made a comeback across the nation during the 1993–94 school year. The issue was ignited in part by the suspension of a Jackson, Mississippi, high school principal who disregarded school district counsel's legal advice and allowed a student to read a prayer over the school's public address system.

Much of the pressure for organized school prayer has been focused at the local level, on school board members and superintendents. By distorting court rulings, religious right groups have sought to pressure school districts into adopting policies that are at odds with the Constitution. On the legislative front, meanwhile, school prayer bills made progress in ten states and the District of Columbia in 1993–94. In addition, the U.S. Congress grappled with the issue as debate over two major education bills was sidetracked by prayer amendments proposed by Sen. Jesse Helms (R.-NC).

The clashes over prayer in the schools involve many of the same issues as attacks on library and classroom materials. In both cases, religious and ideological pressures are brought to bear on school systems, diverting them from their primary tasks of educating children. Often, those who oppose school prayer, like those who support challenged books, are falsely accused of being antireligious or atheistic. Yet, mainstream clergy are attempting to shift the focus of this debate, mounting an increasingly vocal effort to keep organized prayer out of the schools. Their perspective is that government officials should not be editing or approving the content of prayers and that children should not be pressured to participate in religious observances at odds with their own faith.

The Lesson of Censorship

Denying students the educational tools they need to think about and to deal with the complexity of today's society does them an extreme disservice. Perhaps the greater disservice, however, involves the message such action sends to students about their own freedoms. As books and curricula are removed and restricted throughout the nation's schools, children lose the opportunity to learn important lessons. However, the one lesson they do learn—the unfortunate lesson—is that censorship is an appropriate response to controversial ideas.

> *"A study of widely used elementary school social studies texts . . . found that 'religion, traditional values and conservative political and economic positions have been reliably excluded.'"*

The Left Is Censoring Educational Materials

Don Feder and David L. Smith

In Part I of the following two-part viewpoint, syndicated columnist Don Feder responds to charges that the religious right is banning books from public schools. Feder insists that, contrary to these accusations, the left is censoring educational materials by excluding conservative and religious values from books and curricula. In Part II, David L. Smith argues that liberals are more censorious than the religious right. Smith, an art teacher and professional artist, describes numerous instances in which conservative and religious views have been censored while liberal opinions have been protected.

As you read, consider the following questions:

1. What types of sex education programs have been censored by the left, according to Feder?
2. Why does Smith believe liberals will not want their children to read Christmas stories?
3. How do Smith's examples of censorship imply a double standard?

Don Feder, "PAW Wants Only Conservative Books Burned," *Human Events*, October 2, 1993. Reprinted by permission of Don Feder and Creators Syndicate. David Smith, "On Censorship from the Illiberal Left," *St. Croix Review*, April 1993. Reprinted with permission.

I

People for the American Way is at it again—stigmatizing parents who object to public school indoctrination and ignoring blatant censorship on the left.

The media are its accomplices. Each year, the liberal group issues a much-heralded report on attempted book banning in the schools. The survey "paints a picture of public education under siege," PAW's president, Arthur J. Kropp, ominously asserts.

The villain is the left's standard scapegoat. "Religious right groups are far and away the single largest political force promoting censorship," PAW's research director charges.

In its coverage, the media invariably list the most innocuous books to which any idiot has ever objected (*The Wizard of Oz, Of Mice and Men*), creating the impression that this is the norm. They would have us believe that parents who protest the truly odious stuff forced on their children—in the sacred name of AIDS education or multiculturalism—are all bigoted lunatics.

Library books aren't the focal point of parental protest, though some of us prudes don't see why junior high libraries have to carry *Joy of Gay Sex* and *How to Make Love to a Single Woman*.

Over 60% of the instances of censorship, so-called, involve objections to questionable textbooks.

The classics that have come under fire include the "Impressions" series (readers for grades one to six), which promote the New Age and the occult; a controversial drug education program called "Quest," which tells students that they alone can decide whether or not it's okay to use drugs; as well as texts that direct students to fantasize about suicide, attack religion and undermine family authority.

In the famous Tennessee textbook case of the late '80s, parents weren't trying to remove the Holt, Rinehart and Winston series (promoting feminist and other "politically correct" distortions of history) from the schools. They only wanted their children assigned alternative reading. People for the American Way equates this with Nazi book burning.

What Is Censorship?

What is censorship, anyway? If a school refuses to use a science text that presents both evolutionary theory and creationism, has it censored the latter? PAW's position seems to be that censorship (actual or attempted) only occurs if someone objects to a book after it's been adopted.

But by deliberately excluding values they disdain, aren't schools engaging in their own form of censorship? The public education establishment is notoriously biased against literature promoting free enterprise, patriotism, national security and family values.

A study of widely used elementary school social studies texts, sponsored by the National Institute for Education, found that "religion, traditional values and conservative political and economic positions have been reliably excluded."

Why is it censorship to protest educratic elitism? Are the New York parents who objected to first-graders being rainbow-ized by *Daddy's Roommate* and *Heather Has Two Mommies* really wild-eyed fanatics, torches in hand, preparing to *flambe* great literatures?

Convenient Libertarians

PAW's convenient civil libertarians are selective in their defense of besieged books. Under their criteria, public school censorship consists of opposition to texts currently in use. That being the case, how could the organization have overlooked the campaign to purge abstinence-based sex education in its report?

Planned Parenthood is on a mission to proscribe course material that urges teens to save themselves for marriage (cuts down on business at Planned Parenthood abortion clinics). In March 1993, in a suit brought by a lawyer associated with the safe-sex set, a Louisiana district court judge threw out the courses "Sex Respect" and "Facing Reality," in use in the Caddo Parish school system, on the grounds that they taught religion.

Later, the judge modified his ruling. He wasn't actually purging the entire curricula, Judge Frank Thaxton explained. If the school district would excise offensive passages (for instance, the stridently theological comment that "Human reproduction has a higher meaning than animal reproduction"), the law would be satisfied.

The district actually had to go through 1,700 books with black felt-tip pens, inking out forbidden ideas. The result was texts that looked like the letters GIs sent home during World War II. In August, a Planned Parenthood employee managed to have an abstinence curriculum removed from high schools in Modesto, Calif.

By ignoring this and misrepresenting legitimate parental concerns, People for the American Way does it its way: hypocritically, with a hidden agenda and a blind eye toward fashionable book banning.

II

Too often censorship takes on a double standard. Periodically an item on censorship in the boondocks hits the front page of a metropolitan daily much to the amusement of urban sophisticates. Some small-minded school board, for example, wants to ban a recognized work of literary art.

John Steinbeck's *Of Mice and Men* or J.D. Salinger's *Catcher in the Rye* are often the targets of parental wrath, but even such classics as Mark Twain's *Huckleberry Finn* have come under fire. When this happens the total picture often becomes skewed and out of focus. Maybe the ruckus started with a parent suggesting that one book be replaced by another. This is not censorship but an expressed preference. Journalists often let their bias show, and we need to be wary of scare headlines. Out of the millions of books available, only a handful can possibly be used in the classroom. Does that mean that the rejected books are being "censored"?

The Politics of Censorship

In controversies of this sort, politics and values usually play a bigger role than censorship. Conservatives more often than not object to an author's use of "four letter words." Is it unreasonable for a parent not to want his child to be forced to read a book where characters use "swear words" or "dirty words" that would not be tolerated at home?

Liberals are more likely to want to censor the content rather than the specific language of a book. The liberal parent may not want his child to read "Christmas stories" that appear to breach the wall that separates church and state. He may object to books that threaten his "pro-choice" political views even though he is against "pro-choice" when it comes to the freedom to send his child to a private or religious school instead of a public school. He may stand for "political correctness" but it can also mean "political censorship."

It is my contention that the illiberal left is a greater threat to the survival of free speech in this country than is the religious right.

Just how important in the context of freedom-of-speech are liberalized standards for obscenity? Supreme Court Justice William Brennan, certainly no friend of conservatives, wrote that "such utterances are of such slight social value . . . that any benefit that may be derived from them is clearly outweighed by the social interest in order and morality." (*Miller* vs. *California*, 1973)

Double Standards

From the Department of Double Standards let me offer some examples of Censorship from the Illiberal Left:

• Dan Quayle was Vice President of the United States for four years, but, because of a hostile press, we never got to really know him until he spoke before the 1992 Republican Convention in Houston. This is partisan censorship of the meanest kind.

• Airing of a CBS television series pilot of *Driving Miss Daisy* was met with such protests from left wing minority groups that the series was withdrawn. These groups did not want to see a black conservative gentleman portrayed as a hero. In spite of the popularity of the movie, we will not get to see on television a continuation of this story about the loving relationship between a black driver, Hoke, and his elderly white female companion, Miss Daisy.

• At Temple University a group of black students rioted to prevent a conservative black South African speaker from appearing on campus after he had been invited by a faculty member.

• Conservative speakers such as Phyllis Schlafly, Jesse Helms, and Edwin Meese have been greeted at some universities with hoots, howls, and ripe tomatoes. Avowed communists such as Angela Davis have created no problem. The Young American Foundation is trying to overcome this imbalance.

Schools Undermine Religious Beliefs

Education analyst Samuel Blumenfeld contends that school programs supposedly intended to assist students in "clarifying" their values are instead enticing students "to discard the values and religious beliefs of their families and create new sets of values reflecting their own personal desires and leanings, particularly those regarding sex." Many youngsters, for example, have "been encouraged by values clarification to reject the traditional Judeo-Christian prohibitions against sexual perversion and adopt an open and assertive homosexual lifestyle."

Robert W. Lee, *New American*, August 8, 1994.

• A painting of the late Chicago Mayor Harold Washington dressed in women's frilly underwear was angrily ripped from the wall of the Chicago Art Institute by irate city councilmen. They were not reprimanded for this violent sort of censorship. Gross caricatures of Richard Nixon, Ronald Reagan, and Jesse Helms have long been standard fare in contemporary art shows. It depends on whose ox is being gored.

• In Manassas, Virginia, school officials told ten-year-old Audrey Pearson that she could not read her Bible on the school bus.

• Hollywood "stonewalled it" when millions of Christians protested the movie *The Last Temptation of Christ*, yet when one Hopi Indian village complained that the script of the movie *Dark Wind* depicted their ancient rights in a sacrilegious manner, the producer promptly made changes. Christian-bashing is now "in," but Indian-bashing is "out."

• In the state of Florida a school principal felt obliged to use scissors to remove the Bible Club from the high school yearbook.

• Many universities, including Harvard, have banned ROTC

courses on campus, while continuing to receive millions of dollars in government funds.

• The producer of the hit musical *Miss Saigon* was forced to cancel its scheduled U.S. premier because Actors Equity Assoc. refused to permit a white British actor to portray a Eurasian in the show, thus eliminating a popular and job-producing show from the 1990 Broadway season.

• Censorship is at work in a new nonsexist dictionary. Forbidden words include "mankind," "chairwoman," and "housewife." The dictionary suggests that in order not to offend, the word "woman" might be spelled "womyn."

• In 1990 there were 190 cases of students being suspended from public school for distributing religious material.

• A district school superintendent in Spokane banned the singing of the old campfire favorite "Shortnin' Bread" by the chorus when a black fifth-grader complained that it was "insensitive."

• Pete Rose played Ty Cobb in the NBC television movie *Babe Ruth*, but a scene in which Rose appeared wearing a Detroit Tigers uniform was cut because of pressure from Major League Baseball managers.

• In 1985 ABC television spiked its 20/20 segment on the death of Marilyn Monroe because it went into specific detail about the romantic liaisons that Marilyn had with both JFK and Robert Kennedy. In 1992 a PBS series on this subject did cover it in detail.

• The ACLU, while seeking to protect all forms of pornography, seeks to remove all Christian religious displays, such as Christmas nativity scenes, from public parks and buildings. Many would say that the ACLU, an organization whose avowed purpose is to protect our civil liberties, is actually the biggest disseminator of anti-Christian bigotry in the U.S.A.

Intolerance Is Commonplace

What is happening to the right to speak freely on cultural, political, or moral issues? Intolerance for various forms of artistic expression has become commonplace. Will the next step be to remove paintings of The Crucifixion or The Last Supper from The National Gallery in Washington, D.C.? Censorship from the illiberal left takes place quietly and efficiently behind the scenes, while censorship from the religious right becomes a hot topic for ridicule by the media.

The illiberal left has attacked this nation's deepest traditions, has undermined what is organically American: such certitudes as that there is a religious base in life and that there are moral values that are best instilled in the young by mothers and fathers.

"*Speech codes reflect the most blatant and extreme reaction against free expression in the politically correct academy.*"

Campus Speech Codes Violate Free Speech

Patrick M. Garry

Many colleges and universities have adopted speech codes sanctioning speech that is sexist, racist, or offensive in other ways. In the following viewpoint, Patrick M. Garry argues that such regulations are a form of censorship and that they pose a significant threat to First Amendment rights. In trying to impose nonracist and nonoffensive speech on campuses, the author concludes, proponents of speech codes actually make the problem of intolerance worse. Garry is scholar-in-residence at St. John's University in Collegeville, Minnesota, and author of *An American Paradox: Censorship in a Nation of Speech* and *Scrambling for Protection: The New Media and the First Amendment*.

As you read, consider the following questions:

1. In what way do speech codes reveal a "changing view of truth," according to Garry?
2. In the author's view, why will speech codes fail to help solve social problems?
3. How has the self-esteem movement in education contributed to the popularity of speech codes, in Garry's opinion?

Patrick M. Garry, "Censorship by the Free-Speech Generation." Reprinted from *National Forum: The Phi Kappa Phi Journal*, vol. 75, no. 2 (Spring 1995), by permission of the publishers; © by Patrick M. Garry.

Thirty years after the beginnings of the Free Speech Movement at Berkeley, a generational turnaround on censorship seems to have occurred. The politically correct movement has replaced the free-speech movement, and the university is where speech is being most strictly regulated by what was once the free-speech generation. While feminist and civil rights groups previously used their speech freedoms to break down legal and social barriers, many have now turned against those freedoms by supporting speech codes.

Political Correctness and Free Speech

The suffocating effect of political correctness on free speech has been demonstrated by a number of books, [including] Richard Bernstein's *Dictatorship of Virtue*. According to Leon Botstein, president of Bard College, "on many campuses [there is] a culture of forbidden questions." Donald Kagan, a dean at Yale University, has said that at many colleges "there is an imposed conformity of opinion [with] less freedom now than there was [during the days of Joseph McCarthy]."

Not only is the politically correct atmosphere inhibiting free speech on college campuses, but in a complete reversal from the 1960s, First Amendment scholars are focusing more on finding ways to regulate speech than on how to free it. Most academic books on the subject of free speech are critical of Justice Hugo Black's absolutist interpretation of the First Amendment that was so popular on college campuses during the 1960s.

In *Democracy and the Problem of Free Speech*, for instance, Cass Sunstein argues that "currently American law protects much speech that ought not to be protected." Just as Franklin Roosevelt attacked economic laissez-faire, according to Sunstein, the United States must now combat the failure of laissez-faire in the free speech "market." In *There's No Such Thing As Free Speech*, Stanley Fish suggests that any marketplace of ideas inevitably will be managed by government. And in *Only Words*, Catharine MacKinnon argues that censorship is a necessary means for women to achieve equality in a male-dominated society.

Speech Codes and Ideology

Speech codes reflect the most blatant and extreme reaction against free expression in the politically correct academy. Hundreds of colleges have adopted such codes. Donna Shalala, now Secretary of Health and Human Services, presided over the University of Wisconsin as it enacted one of the first university speech codes. Dozens of universities have introduced tough new codes prohibiting speech that leads to, among other things, a "demeaning atmosphere." The University of Michigan, for instance, enacted a code that punishes any speech that stigmatizes or victimizes an individual on the basis of any one of twelve criteria. And the University of Connecticut issued a proclamation banning "inappropriately directed laughter" and "conspicuous exclusion of students from conversations."

The justifications for these codes are the same justifications that have always been used by censors. They present the same arguments used in the 1960s to censor the political radicals. Take, for example, the arguments of Professor Stanley Fish, one of the leading proponents of speech codes. Speech that carries certain undesirable effects, he claims, should not be tolerated. "You must decide whether a university exists primarily as a soap box for free expression or whether it's a workplace based on tasks and obligations that are subject to certain constraints, including verbal constraints," Fish argues, clearly favoring the latter view.

Speech codes not only reveal an increasingly restrictive attitude toward free expression on college campuses, but also reflect a changing view of truth. As educators traditionally have adhered to the idea that truth emerges from a robust marketplace of ideas, free expression has been seen as vital to the pursuit of that truth. In recent years, however, the academic community has taken a more ideological or political view of truth. As Annette Kolodny, dean of the humanities faculty at the University of Arizona admits, "I see my scholarship as an extension of my political activism." And this ideological approach diminishes the importance of free speech. Because truth is predetermined according to one's ideological beliefs, the need for an uninhibited marketplace of ideas no longer exists. Speech is judged by whether it promotes or oppresses a certain politically correct ideology. Consequently, in the political struggles on campuses, tolerance toward speech deemed politically incorrect has declined.

In a politically correct educational environment, the search for truth through free speech is subverted by the belief that what is true is what is ideologically acceptable. This ideological approach, which tries to attain truth through rules about what can and cannot be discussed, undermines the traditional cornerstone of American education—free and open debate. And by becoming more ideological and less tolerant, the university encourages a less civil form of discourse.

A Quick-Fix Mentality

This intolerance of dissident speech reflects the growing political activism of educators. It also, however, reflects the increasing frustrations with the political system and its ability to address certain deep-seated social problems. As political action seems more and more futile in a gridlocked political process, committed activists have turned their attention to the speech expressing various social problems. Speech codes are one result of a quick-fix mentality of impatient advocates who, for instance, argue that racism can be fought by eliminating racist speech. Codes that regulate racist speech are thus an attempt to take quick action on an underlying problem that has proved difficult to solve with remedial social action. According to Robert O'Neil, director of the Thomas Jefferson Center for the Protection of Free Expression, "universities implement speech codes out of a sense of desperation and as a last resort when other approaches prove inadequate."

Liberalism and Free Speech

Liberalism no longer stands unequivocally for free speech. . . . Civil-rights organizations have lobbied successfully to expand civil-rights laws so as to prohibit not only discriminatory conduct but also offensive speech. "Hate speech" laws, stiffer penalties for crimes motivated by racial or ethnic animosity, and campus speech codes are among the best-known examples.

Michael Greve, *National Review*, October 10, 1994.

Censorship of speech in the name of political action, however, is ultimately self-defeating because it inhibits any real action on the underlying social problems. If problems cannot be freely discussed or revealed through speech, they cannot be solved. Consider the analogy of a weed in the lawn. It is easier and temporarily gratifying to cut it down, but unless its roots are pulled out, the weed still lives and grows. So too with social problems: though it may be easier to censor offensive speech, such censorship will not pull out the roots of the underlying problem. Free expression is needed to reveal the social problems, just as the leaves of the weed are needed to show the location of its roots. Without free speech, for instance, the civil rights or feminist movements could never have gotten off the ground.

By suppressing all forms of discriminatory or offensive speech, such codes can have a counterproductive effect, serving to drive prejudices underground, where they can only fester and worsen. Another danger is that speech codes may actually eroticize that which is censored. Forbidden language may be dangerously attractive simply because it is forbidden.

The Therapeutic Culture

In addition to reflecting a quick-fix mentality, speech codes are also a manifestation of the therapeutic culture pervading academe—a side effect of an obsession with self-esteem and psychotherapy. Censorship has become a central component in the vision of the therapeutic state—a state in which no one's feelings or self-esteem is hurt. "The new censors," according to David Lance Goines, author of *The Free Speech Movement: Coming of Age in the 1960s*, "don't want to offend anyone, but that's the whole purpose of free speech."

Self-esteem has become the sacred cow of American culture. It provides the answer to every ill in society, from crime to broken families to educational reform. Speech codes have become a vital weapon in the war against poor self-images. By eliminating offensive speech, the codes can initiate the healing process and encourage the uplifting of self-esteem. Indeed, the drive to implement speech codes mirrors the growth of the self-esteem movement in education.

Like the rest of society, the field of education has become dominated by the therapeutic culture. Intellectual development is yielding to the nurturing of self-esteem as the primary focus of educators. Educators eager to encourage lagging students have decided that raising self-esteem is a sure means of improving their achievement and solving many of the nation's social ills. Women's Studies programs around the country, for instance, are heavily therapized. Such programs, according to Daphne Patai and Noretta Koertge in *Professing Feminism: Cautionary Tales From Inside the Strange World of Women's Studies*, often depict women as victims in need of self-esteem. Likewise, Christine Hoff Sommers has reported that conventions of the National Women's Studies Association Conference are marked by therapeutic uplift and healing rituals, such as holding hands to form "a healing circle" and assuming the posture of trees to gain a feeling of rootedness and tranquility.

Distorting History

The therapeutic culture in education has had a particularly distorting effect on the field of history, because in this field the need to create positive self-images now rivals the quest to discover the truth of the past. Different groups of students are now taught different versions of history, depending on their racial and ethnic identities. Finding that certain minorities have been oppressed throughout history, some historians strive to write history in a way that gives a sense of pride and good self-image to those minorities.

But in pursuing self-esteem, one often leaves truth behind. Afrocentric history, for instance, is an attempt to improve black students' self-esteem by highlighting the accomplishments of African civilization. As an attempt is made to elevate African culture, however, European culture is presented as nothing more than a bastardized version of it. Afrocentrists argue that

Africans were in the New World even before Columbus's journey, that ancient Greece stole its culture from Africa, and that all Western culture derives from Africa.

The need to raise self-esteem is an important goal, but the pursuit of it has had a dark side—the promulgation of speech codes. Although the uplifting of self-esteem has been used to justify these codes, to all censors of every age the goals of their censorship have been worthy goals.

Although censorship has persisted throughout American history, the censorship activities of the sixties generation are particularly troubling. For it was that generation that fought so hard to eliminate censorship, particularly on college campuses. It was that generation that witnessed firsthand the many positive accomplishments of free speech—the civil rights and women's movement and the antiwar protests. Consequently, the turnaround of that generation on free speech shows once again just how fragile those freedoms are.

"Hate-speech codes designed to protect victims are a noble endeavor."

Campus Speech Codes Do Not Violate Free Speech

Lawrence White

Speech codes have been implemented on various college campuses in an attempt to combat derogatory speech. In the following viewpoint, Lawrence White, university counsel at Georgetown University in Washington, D.C., reports that such codes have come under attack in the courts because they have used vague terminology and have been overbroad. White contends that despite these problems, speech codes are a defensible means of protecting the rights of victims of discriminatory harassment. He believes that colleges should adopt new codes that are tailored to withstand challenges in the courts.

As you read, consider the following questions:

1. What four factors should be considered by the authors of the new speech codes, according to Lawrence?
2. According to the author, what message would administrators be sending if they abandoned the effort to create constitutionally acceptable codes?

"Hate-Speech Codes That Will Pass Constitutional Muster" by Lawrence White, *Chronicle of Higher Education*, May 25, 1994; adapted from his paper read at the Stetson University College of Law's National Conference on Law and Higher Education, DeLand, Florida, 1994. Reprinted by permission of the author.

It has been a trying few years for the drafters of hate-speech codes on college and university campuses. The University of Pennsylvania jettisoned its controversial speech code in the fall of 1993 after President Sheldon Hackney, during his confirmation hearing to be Chairman of the National Endowment for the Humanities, questioned whether such codes were the right approach to achieving civility on campus. . . . At Wesleyan University, the University of Michigan, and numerous other institutions, administrators have given up and repealed their codes.

Due largely to the court decisions, we now understand the arguments against campus speech codes: They use inherently vague terminology; they are overbroad, sweeping within their regulatory ambit not only pernicious language, but also language that enjoys constitutional protection. "It is technically impossible to write an anti-speech code that cannot be twisted against speech nobody means to bar," concluded Eleanor Holmes Norton, a former Georgetown University law professor who is now the District of Columbia's Delegate to Congress.

A Noble Endeavor

Despite the problems raised by speech codes, however, we must not forget that there are salutary purposes underlying the effort to draft codes banning derogatory and hurtful epithets. Such codes were intended to serve, and still serve, an important educational purpose: They are expressions of an institution's commitment to the victims of a pernicious and destructive form of behavior. Whenever anybody commits an act or utters a remark that is motivated by hatefulness, it causes harm to a real, flesh-and-blood victim. Hate-speech codes designed to protect victims are a noble endeavor. If institutions abandon the effort to draft policies against hateful speech, they are abandoning the victims the policies were meant to protect.

Campus administrators can learn important lessons from the court cases against the first generation of speech codes. In every instance, the codes that provoked court challenges were ambitiously, almost sweepingly, worded. Several of them, including those at the University of Michigan and the University of Wisconsin, were modeled on the Equal Employment Opportunity Commission's guidelines on sexual harassment. They used concepts and terminology—"intimidating environment for education," "expressed or implied threat to an individual's academic efforts"—awkwardly borrowed from employment law. They treated the university campus as a single, undifferentiated "workplace."

The language they used seemed almost deliberately provocative to civil libertarians—phrases such as "expressive behavior" (University of Wisconsin) and other wording that equated physical behavior with verbal behavior (Central Michigan University)—as though there were no distinction under the First Amendment.

What we have come to refer to as "hate speech" takes many forms on the nation's college campuses. The most prevalent involves remarks by students addressed to other students. For every high-profile case involving a campus speech by Khalid Abdul Muhammad of the Nation of Islam, there are literally dozens, maybe hundreds, of incidents that occur behind the closed doors of dormitory rooms, in dining halls, or in the corridors outside student pubs. We know, regrettably, that a strong correlation exists between hate speech and alcohol abuse.

A Second Generation of Codes

Colleges and universities must now craft a second generation of codes that will serve the important institutional objective of protecting the victims of hateful acts and utterances without violating constitutional principles. These codes would:

• Differentiate between dormitories and classrooms. In an article that appeared in the *Duke Law Journal* in 1990, Nadine Strossen, president of the ACLU, observed that the right to free speech applies with different force in different parts of a college campus. That right, she wrote, "may not be applicable to . . . students' dormitory rooms. These rooms constitute the students' homes. Accordingly, under established free-speech tenets, students should have the right to avoid being exposed to others' expression by seeking refuge in their rooms." A policy that disciplined students for hateful acts or utterances against other students in residence halls would probably bring three-quarters of all hate-speech episodes within the regulatory purview of college administrators without offending traditional free-speech precepts.

• Be tailored to the Supreme Court's decision in *R.A.V.* v. *St. Paul, Minn.* This 1992 decision suggests that anti-discrimination codes are on shaky ground constitutionally if they proscribe some hateful acts or utterances but not others. Any policy that prohibits categories of speech "because of" or "on the basis of" a specific factor—such as race, gender, or sexual orientation—runs the risk of violating the Court's stricture in *R.A.V.* that laws must not single out particular categories of hateful speech for penalties. As ironic as it sounds, the safest hate-speech code may be one that makes no mention of the very groups it is designed to protect.

• Use words emphasizing action and its effects, instead of speech. First Amendment jurisprudence recognizes an important distinction between speech and action and allows a greater degree of latitude when action is being regulated. The first generation of campus speech codes used vocabulary emphasizing speech, which virtually doomed them in advance—for example, they barred certain "comments" or "expressive behavior." By

95

fostering the impression that these policies regulated pure speech, they made an easy target. The receptiveness of courts to arguments that the codes were overbroad—prohibiting speech that should be constitutionally protected along with utterances that deserve no protection (such as yelling "Fire!" in a crowded theater)—requires campuses to be more careful than they were in the past to draft constitutionally acceptable speech codes.

Prohibitions Are Praiseworthy

Prohibiting racially and religiously bigoted speech is praiseworthy because it seeks to elevate, not to degrade, because it draws from human experience, not from woolly dogmas or academic slogans, because it salutes reason as the backbone of freedom and tolerance.

Those who doubt the vicious cycle of hatred derived from verbal assaults against a race or religion should ponder the words of Shylock in "The Merchant of Venice": "If a Jew wrong a Christian, what is his humility? Revenge. If a Christian wrong a Jew, what should his sufferance be by Christian example? Why, revenge. The villainy you teach me, I will execute; and it will go hard but I will better the instruction."

Bruce Fein, *Washington Times*, May 1, 1990.

The second generation of codes should favor "action" vocabulary—prohibiting hostile conduct or behavior that might "incite immediate violence" (the latter being the exact phrasing used in the Supreme Court's half-century-old "fighting words" case, *Chaplinsky* v. *New Hampshire*). Instead of calling them "hate-speech codes," colleges and universities should refer to the new policies as "anti-hate" or "anti-discrimination" codes.
• Enhance the penalties for alcohol-related hate mongering. Most campus conduct codes allow the imposition of disciplinary sanctions for disorderly conduct or violations of drug and alcohol policies. It would be constitutionally defensible to treat hateful acts or utterances as an additional factor to be taken into account when meting out punishment for code violations. For example, a student found guilty of public drunkenness could be sentenced to attend a program designed to treat alcohol abuse, but the same inebriated student could be suspended or expelled for hurling racial epithets or threats at fellow students.

Supporting the Victims of Hate

Drafting a new generation of campus codes to curb hate mongering, codes that zero in on areas of highest risk (dormitories, drunkenness) while avoiding the vagueness and overbreadth that doomed the first generation of codes, is an exercise worth undertaking. Colleges and universities began attempting to regulate hate speech a decade ago for an important reason—to communicate a message of support to the victims of hate. That reason is still compelling today. If institutions abandon the effort to implement constitutionally acceptable codes, they will be sending a message chillingly and accurately expressed by the Stanford University law professor Charles Lawrence in an article that accompanied Ms. Strossen's in the 1990 *Duke Law Journal*:

"I fear that by framing the debate as we have—as one in which the liberty of free speech is in conflict with the elimination of racism—we have advanced the cause of racial oppression and have placed the bigot on the moral high ground, fanning the rising flames of racism."

We all understand civil libertarians' concerns when universities approach the delicate task of regulating certain forms of expressive conduct. But civil libertarians in turn should appreciate the message that is communicated when the rights of insensitive, viciously motivated members of college and university communities are placed above victims' rights to an education untainted by bigoted animosity. By trimming their drafting sails to incorporate the lessons of the first round of court cases, college administrators can satisfy constitutional concerns and at the same time curb the most egregious forms of hate mongering on campus. Then they can send an appropriate message to perpetrator and victim alike: Hateful utterances and behavior are repugnant forms of conduct that colleges and universities will not tolerate.

"Many . . . professional editors believe that the Hazelwood *decision has had only a marginal impact on high school newspapers. Evidently, none of them have been reading any high school newspapers lately."*

The *Hazelwood* Decision Has Resulted in Censorship

Joel Kaplan

In 1988 the Supreme Court decided in the case of *Hazelwood School District v. Kuhlmeier* that school officials have the right to prevent high school journalists from publishing offensive material. In the following viewpoint, Joel Kaplan argues that the *Hazelwood* decision has had a chilling effect on high school journalism. He details a number of examples of newspapers that have had to kill stories at the request of their school administrations. Kaplan is an assistant professor of newspaper journalism at the S.I. Newhouse School of Public Communications at Syracuse University in New York.

As you read, consider the following questions:

1. On what basis did many newspaper editors agree with the Supreme Court's decision in the *Hazelwood* case, according to Kaplan?
2. What do the author's various examples have in common? How do they constitute censorship?

Joel Kaplan, "*Hazelwood* Decision Continues to Haunt High School Journalists," *Editor and Publisher*, May 7, 1994. Reprinted by permission of the author.

It has been more than six years since the Supreme Court handed down its decision severely limiting the freedom of the high school press.

Perhaps the most unconscionable aspect of this decision was the acquiescence by professional journalists.

Throughout the country, editorialists supported the Supreme Court's decision, declaring that high school journalists lack the maturity and responsibility to handle complete First Amendment freedoms.

Many newspaper editors agreed with the Supreme Court because they said the school principal is the publisher of the school paper and therefore has the right to do as he or she pleases with it.

Many of those same professional editors believe that the *Hazelwood* decision has had only a marginal impact on high school newspapers. Evidently, none of them have been reading any high school newspapers lately.

The *Tattler*

In the fall of 1993, students at Ithaca (N.Y.) High School discovered that one of their teachers had been arrested for allegedly growing marijuana. The students, two freshmen, did what any good journalists would do. They examined police and court records relating to the arrest and then asked some students at the school their reaction.

The article prepared for the student paper, the *Tattler*, was headlined, "Teacher Arrested for Possession of Drugs" followed by a lowercase "What Does IHS Think About It?" by Kyle Jarrow and Sara Kotmel.

This is how the article began:

"On September 14, Christine Wilbur of 277 Lake Road, King Ferry, and her boyfriend, Martin Allen, were arrested for growing 612 plants of marijuana (a Class A misdemeanor) at their home. Wilbur, a special education teacher at IHS, was released on a court appearance ticket."

The article goes on to say that sheriff's deputies found that the marijuana weighed more than eight ounces, so they were attempting to change the charge from a misdemeanor to a felony, and that the case was before the grand jury. The article concludes by quoting the reactions of several students.

Though the students had planned to publish the article in their October edition, IHS Principal Mark Piechota refused to allow it to run.

The newspaper's adviser, Eileen Bach, who brought me a copy of the story, said she knew from a journalistic perspective that the article should run because it was legitimate news of interest to students. But she said she was uncomfortable running the article because she knew the teacher and did not want to add to her pain.

Censoring Sexual Topics

The arbitrary censorship that exists under *Hazelwood* began almost immediately. . . .

Sexual topics are frequently deemed to be "inappropriate" for a high school audience. In some cases, the desire to suppress discussions about sex overcomes common sense as well as respect for free speech—as when a high school superintendent in Arizona removed any mention of sexual transmission from an article about AIDS.

Kimberly Phillips, *EXTRA!*, March/April 1994.

Bach said she told the student editor that she would take the article to the principal and let him make the final decision. Bach said Piechota refused to allow the article to run in the school paper.

Citing *Hazelwood*, she said, Piechota told her that the article would make it impossible for Wilbur to continue to be an effective teacher.

When contacted about why he killed the story, Piechota at first said, "I don't want to talk about it."

The principal eventually called back to explain his position:

"It was because the article concerned a staff member and there were legal proceedings involving the staff member. I didn't want to jeopardize those proceedings. I thought printing the article would undermine her ability to teach, and I have to maintain order in the building."

Other Cases

Piechota used the *Hazelwood* decision to kill a legitimate news story. But he is not by far the only high school principal to censor high school journalists. Among the incidents in the past few years:

• A Fort Wayne, Ind., principal killed an article that meticulously detailed how the girls' tennis coach improperly pocketed $1,400 that team members had paid for court time. The principal told students that the article was factual, accurate and not libelous. He then made a deal with the tennis coach that if the coach resigned, the article would not run in the student paper.

• After a high school senior in Gahanna, Ohio, passed out and nearly died from alcohol poisoning in an early morning math class, the high school newspaper wanted to print a story about teen drinking without mentioning the girl's name. The vice principal killed the generic story because it might be traumatic to the girl.

• In Rockford, Ill., the high school paper was barred from reporting about the arrest of the high school football coach on charges of sexual assault. The local newspaper wrote details of the arrest and subsequent guilty plea, but the principal said the topic was off limits to the school paper because the teacher's wife continued to work at the school.

• In Manchester, N.H., the high school principal shut down the paper after it printed an editorial questioning a decision by a teacher not to release vote totals in a student election.

Denied the Basics of Good Journalism

These incidents and many more are detailed in a new book about high school journalism published by the Freedom Forum. The book, *Death by Cheeseburger: High School Journalism in the 1990s and Beyond*, should be required reading for all professional newspaper editors.

If they read it, they might discover that their pool of future reporters and editors is ill-equipped to combat government secrecy and corruption because they never learned the basic principles of good journalism in high school.

A Good Lesson

Actually, the lessons of high school censorship were delivered much better by the editors of the Ithaca High School newspaper.

They published this editorial in response to the killing of the drug arrest story:

"The rumors that are started, however, when students learn about incidents from outside sources are much worse than the actual truth.

"As a school newspaper, the *Tattler* has responsibilities to the readers: Relaying the truth of an event or action in a fair and unbiased manner. Unfortunately, this is a difficult responsibility to meet when the administration forbids any controversial article.

"Ironically, even this editorial has been censored, which is why certain incidents are merely alluded to. Not only may particular names not be written but references to specific events are not permitted.

"It doesn't look like things are going to change, at least not until the Supreme Court reverses their decision and mandates that all constitutional rights are extended to school newspapers. Until that time, however, don't look at the *Tattler* for any earth-shattering news stories."

==========

"The current study provides corroborating evidence from student editors that the Hazelwood *decision has not reduced scholastic press freedom as was expected."*

==========

The *Hazelwood* Decision Has Not Resulted in Censorship

Thomas V. Dickson

The 1988 Supreme Court decision *Hazelwood School District v. Kuhlmeier* gave high school officials the right to intervene in student publications. In the following viewpoint, Thomas V. Dickson describes a study he conducted on the effects of the *Hazelwood* decision on high school journalists. He concludes that the press freedoms of high school journalism have not been unduly restricted by the decision. Dickson is associate professor of journalism at Southwest Missouri State University.

As you read, consider the following questions:

1. How did the author conduct his study?
2. What conclusions did the author reach concerning the effect of the *Hazelwood* decision? What are the implications of his findings for high school journalists?

Excerpted from "Self-Censorship and Freedom of the Public High School Press" by Thomas V. Dickson, *Journalism Educator*, September 22, 1994. Reprinted with permission.

For more than 25 years, researchers harbored three basic assumptions about the scholastic press: a) that school officials have shown little respect for student journalists' First Amendment rights; b) that student journalists are too deferential to school authorities; and c) that the student press tends to avoid controversial topics.

Researchers expected to find that the situation had worsened after the Supreme Court's 1988 *Hazelwood School District* v. *Kuhlmeier* decision, which allowed school officials to censor school-sponsored publications that are not public forums and to muzzle the speech of faculty members. Research following the ruling suggested that was not the case, however.

Post-*Hazelwood* researchers found that high school principals and publications advisers did not see much change in the amount of student-newspaper censorship following the ruling. Critics of such research, however, say that these results are based upon arguably biased reports. They also suggest that unpublished prohibitions on content, pressure on student journalists, intimidation and student deference often negate the need for overt censorship. Kay Phillips surmised the following from her pre- and post-*Hazelwood* study of North Carolina high schools:

> In all schools, advisers exert subtle pressure and, in practice, most of them are censors by the definition applied in this study: both cutting controversial material and instituting a policy or atmosphere of intimidation that causes students to refrain from printing certain materials in the school newspaper. Clearly, persistent student editor deference to such authority has a stultifying effect on the student press.

Post-*Hazelwood* researchers usually have studied only censorship and have been unable to determine if *self*-censorship is a problem for the scholastic press. Neither have they determined why press freedom did not suffer after the *Hazelwood* ruling. Their research points out the need for a reassessment of the extent of press freedom at U.S. public high schools. It also identifies a need to study factors associated with scholastic press freedom. . . .

Research Questions

This study proposed two research questions about censorship and self-censorship of the high school press:

1. Do student editors and advisers agree about the extent to which self-censorship and censorship are taking place at public high school newspapers?

2. To what extent are the adviser's journalism training and advising experience related to the amount of self-censorship as well as censorship reported?

The sample, which consisted of 1,040 high schools, was generated randomly by Educational Directories, Inc. by computer from a list of all public high schools in the country. In April 1992, a cover letter, a 32-question survey addressed to the student newspaper editor, and a self-addressed business reply envelope were sent to each school in the sample. A follow-up mailing was sent three weeks later.

A total of 426 surveys were returned (41%). Of that number, 323 were completed by student editors; these were analyzed. A total of 103 returned surveys were unusable or were returned by schools without a student newspaper. These were not analyzed.

In early May, 35-question surveys addressed to the student newspaper adviser were sent to the same sample of 1,040 schools. A follow-up letter was sent to those who did not respond. A total of 387 surveys were returned (37%). Of that number, 270 were from advisers and were analyzed. A total of 117 were from schools without a student newspaper or were otherwise unusable. . . .

Questions in this study were intended to gather information about the use of prior review, censorship (defined in this study as prior restraint), and student self-restraint taking place as well as the existence of possible causes of self-censorship (including pressure, intimidation, and student deference). Respondents were asked what had taken place at the school during that school year. They also were asked their opinion of the *Hazelwood* ruling.

Three community/school characteristics (region of the country, community size, and school size) were analyzed, as were five newspaper characteristics (whether the newspaper was a credit or non-credit class, how often the newspaper was published, presence of a school publication policy, type of publication policy, and source of the publication policy).

Advisers' responses were analyzed based upon four individual characteristics: gender, number of college journalism course hours, years of journalism advising experience, and membership in journalism organizations. . . .

Editors and Advisers Agree

Respondents. No statistically significant difference was found between the 1992 editor and adviser samples based upon seven of the independent variables investigated. The only statistically significant difference concerned the source of the publication policy. Student editors were more likely than advisers to think that students were the source of the policy; however, that difference likely can be attributed to students' misperceptions about policies put into effect in previous years.

Just over one-fourth of the advisers and just under one-sixth of the student editors had no opinion about the *Hazelwood* ruling. Student editors, however, were more likely to disagree with the ruling than were advisers. Of those respondents who expressed an opinion, 81 percent of student editors and 69 percent of advisers disagreed with the ruling.

Responses of advisers and editors to most other questions on the survey were quite similar. . . .

Research questions. The answer to the first research question ("Do student editors and advisers agree about the extent to which self-censorship and censorship are taking place at public high school newspapers?") is "Yes, for the most part." While some differences were found, editors and advisers agreed that censorship and self-censorship were not taking place very often and they did not appear to be keeping most newspapers from covering important or controversial issues.

Table 1 compares advisers' and student editors' responses to several questions about prior review and prior restraint. Responses by both advisers and editors indicated that nearly all advisers looked at the newspaper before publication. While 19 in 20 advisers used prior review often or always, only about one-third of principals had ever used it. Despite the high use of prior review by advisers, prior restraint had been used in only a minority of schools surveyed, and then rarely.

The difference between responses of advisers and student editors was statistically significant on three of nine questions about prior review and restraint: whether the adviser read the newspaper before publication, whether the adviser had withheld a story because of the topic, and whether the adviser had rejected an ad because of topic. In all three cases, student editors were significantly less likely than advisers to indicate prior review or prior restraint had taken place. Thus, when differences existed, editors reported more freedom than did advisers.

Table 1
Editors' and Advisers' Responses to
Survey Questions on Aspects of Censorship

	Editor	Adviser

Prior Review

1. Does the adviser read the contents of the newspaper before it is published?

	Editor	Adviser
Never/a few times	5%	5%
Fairly/quite often	13%	6%
Always	82%	89%

2. Does the principal read the contents of the newspaper before it is published?

	Editor	Adviser
Never	62%	64%
A few times	21%	22%
Fairly often/quite often/always	17%	14%

Prior Restraint

1. Has adviser told the editor he/she couldn't run a particular editorial?

```
No...................................................79%    73%
Yes..................................................21%    27%
```

2. Has adviser withheld an editorial from publication or required that it be substantially rewritten (other than for style and grammar mistakes or factual errors) because of the subject matter?

```
No...................................................63%    65%
Yes..................................................37%    35%
```

3. Has adviser told the editor he/she couldn't run a particular story?

```
No...................................................64%    70%
Yes..................................................36%    30%
```

4. Has the adviser changed copy without telling the editor he/she was going to do so?

```
No...................................................76%    71%
Yes..................................................24%    29%
```

5. Has the adviser withheld a news story from publication or required that it be substantially rewritten (other than for style and grammar mistakes or factual errors) because of the subject matter?

```
No...................................................74%    65%
Yes..................................................26%    35%
```

6. Has the adviser rejected advertising because of the subject matter?

```
No...................................................83%    67%
Yes..................................................17%    33%
```

7. Has the principal ever told the adviser or the editor that a story or editorial couldn't run or would have to be changed before it could run?

```
No...................................................66%    63%
Yes..................................................34%    37%
```

Self-Censorship

Table 2 compares student editors' and advisers' responses to questions concerning aspects of self-censorship. Only a small percentage of advisers and student editors (less than 15% in all cases) reported much pressure by the adviser before publication, but a considerable number of student editors indicated a potential for deference.

About half of the editors (51%) stated that they would get into trouble if they wanted to print something about a controversial topic. Most of them thought the problem would be with school officials, however, and not with the adviser.

Most student editors (68%) stated that it was fairly or very important to them whether the adviser would find a story to be objectionable. On the other hand, most advisers (91%) stated that they did not worry much or at all that the newspaper might include controversial stories.

For the three questions for which responses of advisers and editors were significantly different, editors were more likely than advisers to worry about controversial contents.

Table 2
Editors' and Advisers' Responses to Survey Questions on Aspects of Self-Censorship

Editor *Adviser*

Adviser Pressure

1. How much has the adviser stressed to the editor that stories about controversial subjects should not go into the newspaper?

	Editor	Adviser
Not at all	45%	49%
Not much	40%	43%
Fairly much/quite a bit	15%	8%

2. Has adviser suggested that editor not publish an editorial because it was too controversial (without actually telling editor not to run it)?

	Editor	Adviser
Never	67%	64%
A few times	31%	35%
Fairly often/quite often	2%	1%

3. Has adviser suggested that editor not publish a story because it was too controversial (without actually saying "don't run this")?

	Editor	Adviser
No	66%	65%
A few times	33%	34%
Fairly/quite often	1%	1%

Student Deference

1. Would editor get into trouble with adviser or with school official for wanting to print something about a controversial topic?

	Editor	Adviser
Yes, with adviser, maybe school officials	12%	12%
Yes, with school officials, but not adviser	39%	28%
No	49%	60%

2. When deciding whether to assign or use a story, how important is it to the editor whether the adviser will find it objectionable?

	Editor	Adviser
Not important or not very important	32%	28%
Fairly important	47%	48%
Very important	21%	24%

3. How much does the adviser worry that the newspaper might include controversial stories?

	Editor	Adviser
Not at all	21%	28%
Not much	51%	63%
Fairly much/quite a bit	28%	9%

Self-Restraint

1. Do student reporters hold off from doing stories about potentially controversial subjects because such stories might be seen as objectionable by the adviser?

	Editor	Adviser
Never	40%	35%

Once in a while 50%   55%
Fairly often/quite often 10%   10%

2. Has editor withheld an editorial from publication because he/she thought the topic was too controversial?

Never 76%   73%
A few times 23%   24%
Fairly/quite often 1%   3%

3. Has editor withheld a story from publication because he/she thought the topic was too controversial?

Never 79%   74%
A few times 20%   25%
Fairly/quite often 1%   1%

4. Has newspaper failed to run important stories because editor didn't think he/she would be allowed to print them?

Never 60%   58%
A few times 35%   38%
Fairly/quite often 5%   4%

Table 2 also shows results of questions about students' use of self-restraint. No statistically significant disagreement was found between advisers and editors concerning the amount of self-restraint being used. Half of the student editors stated that reporters occasionally avoided controversial topics because the adviser might find such topics objectionable. Only one-tenth of the editors thought it happened very often, however. A majority of editors (60%) stated that their newspapers had not failed to run important stories due to fear of prior restraint.

The Effects of Training and Experience

The second research question was: "To what extent are the adviser's journalism training and advising experience related to the amount of self-censorship as well as censorship reported?" To answer the question, [the importance of several variables were calculated] based upon responses to questions concerning aspects of censorship and self-censorship. . . .

Three adviser characteristics were directly related to disagreement with the *Hazelwood* ruling: in excess of six hours college journalism classes, more than five years of advising experience, and membership in one or more journalism professional organizations. Schools with advisers reporting those characteristics did not always have less censorship and self-censorship, however.

The more advising experience the adviser reported, the less likely the principal was to look at the newspaper before its publication. Advisers with more experience, however, were more likely to have suggested that the editor not publish a story because it was too controversial, to have withheld a story because it was too controversial, and to have rejected a controversial advertisement.

Advisers with more college course hours in journalism were more likely to state that student reporters avoided controversial stories because the adviser might object and to state that the editor had withheld a controversial story. In addition, such advisers were more likely to have rejected an advertisement because of subject matter.

Freedom Has Not Been Reduced

The current study provides corroborating evidence from student editors that the *Hazelwood* decision has not reduced scholastic press freedom as was expected in 1988. The study also found that most editors were deferential to the adviser; however, editors and advisers agreed that only limited self-censorship was being practiced and that most newspapers had not failed to run important stories because of self-censorship.

The results of this study present a question and a challenge for college and university journalism educators. On one hand, the study found that advisers with more college journalism course hours and with more advising experience were more likely to disagree with the *Hazelwood* ruling. On the other hand, it found that advisers who had taken more college journalism courses or who had more advising experience sometimes were more likely than their less-educated and less-experienced counterparts to use prior restraint.

It also appears that more knowledgeable and better trained advisers tend to intimidate their students more than poorly trained, inexperienced ones and that their students tend to be more deferential. Thus, their student editors may be more likely to use self-censorship.

Journalism educators may ask themselves how they can best teach future high school journalism teachers and advisers to find the proper balance between good journalism and free expression. While adviser characteristics do not appear as important to press freedom as the high school's stand on student freedom of expression, the position taken by the adviser is important in a time when restrictions on student First Amendment rights have been given the imprimatur of the Supreme Court.

Periodical Bibliography

The following articles have been selected to supplement the diverse views presented in this chapter. Addresses are provided for periodicals not indexed in the *Readers' Guide to Periodical Literature*, the *Alternative Press Index*, the *Social Sciences Index*, or the *Index to Legal Periodicals and Books*.

Jonathan Chait — "Backfire on Campus," *American Prospect*, Summer 1995. Available from PO Box 383080, Cambridge, MA 02138-3080.

Richard Delgado — "Hateful Speech, Loving Communities: Why Our Notion of 'a Just Balance' Changes So Slowly," *California Law Review*, July 1994.

Bonnie Dricson — "Banned in U.S.A.: Reference Guide to Book Censorship in Schools and Public Libraries," *English Journal*, January 1996. Available from NCTE, 1111 Kenyon Rd., Urbana, IL 61801.

Dave Gentry — "Full Circle for the Berkeley Free Speech Movement," *New York Times*, December 2, 1994.

Scott Gottlieb — "There's No Such Thing as Justice on Campus," *USA Today*, March 1995.

Debra Gersh Hernandez — "Censorship in the Schools," *Editor and Publisher*, September 16, 1995. Available from 11 W. 19th St., New York, NY 10011.

Franklyn G. Jenifer — "Hate Speech Is Still Free Speech," *New York Times*, May 13, 1994.

Michael J. Laird — "The Constitutionality of Political Correctness," *Communications and the Law*, September 1994.

John Leo — "Campus Affirmatively Favors Censorship," *Conservative Chronicle*, January 1, 1996. Available from PO Box 29, Hampton, IA 50441.

James L. Payne — "Education Versus the American Way," *National Review*, September 25, 1995.

Joannie M. Schrof — "The Costly Price of Free Speech," *U.S. News & World Report*, May 16, 1994.

Harvey A. Silvergate — "P. C. Gags Fair Harvard," *National Law Journal*, January 8, 1996.

Are Stronger Antipornography Laws Needed?

CENSORSHIP

Chapter Preface

When photography student Toni Marie Angeli went to pick up photographs of her son from a photo lab in Cambridge, Massachusetts, in February 1996, she was met by two plainclothes police detectives who arrested her for child pornography. The photo lab had reported Angeli for taking pictures of a nude child.

Angeli, who was never formally charged with child abuse or pornography, claimed her First Amendment rights were violated. However, Catherine Walsh, a columnist for *America* magazine, reports that public opinion in Cambridge weighed heavily against Angeli. According to Walsh, many in the community sided with the photo lab after some of the photographs were shown on a local news program. She writes that

> the ones shown on the news were close-up shots of a naked child in various poses, looking uncomfortable and self-conscious. Not shown, but widely reported and discussed, were photos of the child urinating outdoors or being dragged across a fully clothed man's chest.

Walsh concludes that the photo-lab workers, who were unaware that the man was the child's father and that the photographs were taken by the child's mother, were "wise to call the police." She contends that the risks posed by child pornography outweigh whatever infringement the photo lab's actions imposed on Angeli's First Amendment rights.

Walsh and others believe that the potential harm of pornography—especially to children—justifies governmental action to restrict the production and distribution of such materials. However, as the Angeli case demonstrates, it is often difficult to determine whether a particular image is pornographic or harmful. Some fear that in its zeal to protect children, the state could become excessively repressive and intrusive. This view is held by Marilyn Zimmerman, a Wayne State University art professor who was subjected to criminal proceedings after a nude photograph of her three-year-old daughter was found in her wastebasket. Zimmerman maintains that the investigation was "an incredible violation of everything I stand for. The innocent image of a little girl owning and enjoying her own body became the template for shameful cultural projections of sexuality."

The viewpoints in this chapter weigh the relative merits of protecting those who might be harmed by pornography against the right to free speech. The writers address both the wisdom of enacting laws against pornography and the projected difficulties, benefits, and side effects of such laws.

"Congress needs to enact a statutory regime that will create strong incentives against distributing child pornography."

Stronger Child Pornography Laws Are Needed

Matthew S. Queler

In the following viewpoint, Matthew S. Queler argues that the current child pornography law is ineffective because it allows distributors to avoid liability. He advocates a new law that eliminates this weakness in the current law and that contains stiff sanctions against distributors of obscene child pornography. Queler insists that such legislation would not unduly infringe on distributors' constitutional right to free speech. If any chilling of speech did occur, according to Queler, it would be justified by the need to protect children from the harms that result from the production and distribution of child pornography. Queler is a contributor to the *Harvard Journal of Law & Public Policy*.

As you read, consider the following questions:

1. What kind of conduct is outlawed by section 2252 of the Child Protection Act of 1984 as quoted by Queler?
2. Why is it essential to attack the child pornography industry from the distribution side, in the author's opinion?
3. According to Queler, why will the regulations he proposes not have a chilling effect?

Matthew S. Queler, "The Increased Need for Stronger Anti-Child Pornography Statutes in the Wake of *United States v. X-Citement Video, Inc.*, 115 S. Ct. 464 (1994)." Excerpted and reprinted with permission from the *Harvard Journal of Law & Public Policy* 18: 929–44 (Summer 1995). Copyright 1995, Harvard Society for Law & Public Policy, Inc.

"Of all the crimes known to our society, perhaps none is more revolting than the sexual exploitation of children, particularly for the purpose of producing child pornography." Few would disagree with the House Judiciary Committee's 1986 condemnation of child pornography. As a result, when the child pornography industry boomed in the 1970s, Congress enacted legislation to combat the interstate trafficking of such material. The Child Protection Act of 1984 (CPA) further facilitated the prosecution of child pornographers. However, section 2252, which targeted the distribution of child pornography, was poorly written. It was ambiguous with respect to the scienter requirements [requirements to prove the accused acted with knowledge of committing an offense] for the elements of the offense. As a result of this ambiguity, federal judges have struggled to determine the proper reading of the statute and often have come to conflicting conclusions.*

In *United States v. X-Citement Video, Inc.* (1994), the Supreme Court resolved the confusion by interpreting the statute to require the government to prove knowledge for each element of the offense. The Court interpreted section 2252 in the only way that preserves both the constitutionality and rationality of the statute. A superior decision would have been to invalidate the statute. Congress should rewrite section 2252 to encourage distributors to take steps to ensure that they do not traffic in child pornography. . . .

Under the Court's interpretation of section 2252, a defendant may avoid criminal liability simply by ignoring indications that he is engaged in illicit transactions. As interpreted by the majority, the statute now fails to impose the proper incentives on distributors to act affirmatively to ensure that they do not deal in child pornography.

Strict liability, on the other hand, creates strong incentives for

---

* Section 2252 provides in pertinent part:
   (a) any person who—
   (1) knowingly transports or ships in interstate or foreign commerce by any means including by computer or mails any visual depiction, if—
   (A) the producing of such visual depiction involves the use of a minor engaging in sexually explicit conduct; and
   (B) such visual depiction is of such conduct;
   (2) knowingly receives, or distributes any visual depiction that has been mailed, or has been shipped or transported in interstate or foreign commerce, or which contains materials which have been mailed or so shipped or transported, by any means including by computer, or knowingly reproduces any visual depiction for distribution in interstate or foreign commerce by any means including by computer or through the mails, if—
   (A) the producing of such visual depiction involves the use of a minor engaging in sexually explicit conduct; and
   (B) such visual depiction is of such conduct. . . .
   There are three elements of the offense to which a scienter requirement may apply: (1) the transporting, shipping, receiving, or distributing of any visual depiction; (2) the nature and contents of the material; and (3) the age of the performer or person depicted.

parties to ensure that the proscribed activity does not occur. "In the interest of the larger good, [a strict liability offense] puts the burden of acting at hazard upon a person otherwise innocent but standing in responsible relation to a public danger," [according to *United States v. Dotterweich*, (1943)]. Furthermore, according to Laurie L. Levenson, strict liability effectively eliminates the "possibility that a culpable defendant would escape punishment by feigning ignorance or mistake." Strict liability for distributors of sexually explicit material, however, poses problems. Distributors lack the opportunity to deal with the depicted performers personally and therefore would have great difficulty ascertaining the performers' ages. In addition, distributors deal in vast quantities of materials, so it would be "virtually impossible for them to know the contents" of everything they distribute, according to Robert R. Strang. As the Ninth Circuit stated, "it would undoubtedly chill the distribution of books and films if sellers were burdened with learning not only the content of all of the materials they carry but also the ages of actors with whom they have had no direct contact." Therefore, holding distributors to a pure strict liability standard with respect to the age of the performer might be unconstitutionally overbroad because it might have a substantial chilling effect on expression protected by the First Amendment.

A Strong Regime Is Needed

Congress needs to enact a statutory regime that will create strong incentives against distributing child pornography, but which does not discourage the distribution of constitutionally protected materials. Two changes should be instituted to move in this direction. First, Congress needs to fill a gap in the current regime. Congress has enacted federal laws prohibiting the distribution of obscenity, and although section 2252 prohibits the distribution of child pornography, no law specifically targets obscene child pornography. Congress therefore should enact a statute that outlaws the distribution of obscene child pornography, holds a defendant strictly liable with respect to the age of the performer, and contains stiffer sanctions than either the statutes that prohibit obscenity in general or section 2252. Because the distribution of obscenity already is prohibited by federal law, the new statute simply would provide for increased penalties if the illegal obscenity also depicts underage performers. This statute would be constitutional, as it would not chill protected speech any more than the general obscenity statutes. Furthermore, . . . once a defendant is shown to have sold obscene materials illegally, the fact that the depicted performer was underage may be considered in increasing the defendant's punishment, regardless of whether the defendant knew of this fact.

This statute would send a strong message to would-be distributors of child pornography. "[S]trict liability expresses emphatically that such conduct will not be tolerated regardless of the actor's intent," according to Levenson. Moreover, holding a defendant strictly liable for the age of the performer would simplify child pornography prosecutions. This simplification would create a risk of steeper criminal sanctions for distributors of child obscenity and would serve as a better deterrent than the current statutes. Any increase in deterrence would be valuable because child pornography undoubtedly causes unspeakable harms. Finally, much of child pornography "would be found obscene under existing federal and state obscenity laws," according to H.L.A. Hart. Therefore, Congress could enact this penalty-enhancing statute, which would proscribe the distribution of most of the material currently defined as child pornography, while simultaneously holding distributors strictly liable with respect to the age of the performer.

Revising Section 2252

Second, Congress needs to rewrite section 2252. The Food, Drug and Cosmetic Act (FDCA) provides a useful framework. The FDCA prohibits the mislabeling or adulteration of food or drugs and the introduction of such articles into interstate commerce. Merely causing a prohibited act, regardless of fault, is a violation. This strict liability applies to distributors and any persons in responsible relation to a violation. Nonetheless, "a person who introduces an illegal article into commerce is exempt from liability if he has received the article in good faith and obtained a written guaranty that it is not in violation of the Act.". . .

A revised section 2252 should be modeled after the statutory regime found in food and drug law. The statute should impose strict liability on a distributor with respect to the age of the performer or person visually depicted. The distributor should be exempted from criminal liability if: (1) he obtains, in good faith, a written guarantee from the producer that all people depicted as engaging in sexually explicit conduct are not minors; and (2) a reasonable distributor would have been satisfied that the guarantee was legitimate and would not have investigated further to determine whether the guarantee was given falsely. . . .

Because the child pornography industry effectively is part of the underground economy, it is essential to attack it from the distribution side. Requiring distributors to obtain a guarantee creates an opportunity for indicia of illicit dealings to present themselves. And because distributors would face criminal liability for ignoring or missing obvious signals of questionable transactions, they would have an incentive against "feigning indifference or mistake."

A statute with these amendments would be much stronger than section 2252 as interpreted by the Court in *X-Citement Video*, and would be constitutional. The major problem with a pure strict liability standard would be the chilling effect on distributors of non-obscene adult pornography. In such a regime, distributors would need to try to obtain the ages of all the performers in sexually explicit material—a requirement that most believe is too burdensome. The regime suggested here does not pose the same problem as it is narrowly tailored to serve the government's interest. The burden on distributors of protected expression would be minimal. Producers of sexually explicit material already are required to ascertain and record the ages of its performers. As in the case of food and drug producers, it would require very little effort on the part of pornography producers to provide a written guarantee that their product complies with the applicable statutes. In most cases, this guarantee would satisfy the distributor's burden, because there generally would be no reason for the distributor to doubt the guarantee's legitimacy, especially when the producer is known within the industry. Thus, this requirement rarely will be more burdensome than obtaining and retaining a sales receipt.

DeOre, ©1986 The Dallas Morning News. Reprinted with permission of Universal Press Syndicate. All rights reserved.

In transactions in which certain indications suggest that the proffered guarantee may be false, the distributor merely needs to ask the producer to provide a copy of the records documenting the performers' ages. Compliance with such a request would cost little, and then a reasonable distributor would satisfy her statutory duty, having no reason to believe the guarantee was false. The distributor, therefore, would face little risk of being found criminally liable. Because a distributor could, in most cases, satisfy her duty of care with little effort, this new regime would not, in the words of Janelle E. Pretzer, "significantly compromise the exercise of constitutionally protected speech in a substantial number of instances," and therefore would pass constitutional muster.

If any chilling does occur, it would be a rare situation in which the producer, for whatever reason, could not adequately reassure the distributor that the depictions were not of children. Any such chilling, however, would be de minimis and would be outweighed by the substantial government interests involved. Pornography is low value speech that does not receive full First Amendment protection. Balanced against this interest is the protection of children, an "objective of surpassing importance," the Court ruled in *New York v. Ferber* (1984).

"The need for special protection of the young has become an accepted government interest," according to Strang. Statutory rape laws hold defendants strictly liable for the age of their partner despite the strong presumption against strict liability for non-public welfare offenses and for felonies. Furthermore, according to Potuto, "many jurisdictions today make it a criminal offense to fail to report a suspected instance of child abuse or child sex abuse. . . . Several jurisdictions expressly cover child sexual exploitation . . . in the list of crimes for which observers have an affirmative duty to report" even though there generally is no duty to act to prevent a crime. Concededly, the First Amendment does not speak to these examples. The government's interest in protecting children, however, has justified a number of infringements on First Amendment interests that would not have been otherwise permitted. Moreover, the First Amendment already has given way to the protection of children in the context of child pornography. Private, in-home possession of child pornography may be criminalized, while private, in-home possession of obscene adult material may not be. Similarly, child pornography may be barred even if it does not appeal to prurient interests or is not patently offensive, and may be barred without considering the work as a whole, while adult pornography cannot be. The need for protecting our children today should be no less compelling than the reasons found to protect them in the past.

119

"If national attention is to be focused on defining child pornography, what we need is not a hasty stitching together of legislation . . . but an informed conversation."

Stronger Child Pornography Laws Are Not Needed

Marjorie Garber and Amy Adler

In the following two-part viewpoint, Marjorie Garber and Amy Adler argue that erotic images of children are widespread in the popular culture. In Part I, Garber, the author of *Vested Interests: Cross-Dressing and Cultural Anxiety*, suggests that instead of responding to this phenomenon with new child pornography laws, the public should engage in an informed discussion about such images. In Part II, Amy Adler, a New York City attorney, contends that child pornography laws may actually encourage rather than reduce the production of pornographic images of children.

As you read, consider the following questions:

1. According to Garber, what do civil libertarians believe will happen if stronger child pornography laws are passed?
2. What are the motives of those who advocate harsher child pornography laws, in Garber's opinion?
3. According to Adler, what happens when the government cracks down on child pornography?

I

For a moment in November 1993 it seemed as if the White House, under pressure from conservatives, was about to propose a broad new "child pornography" statute banning some depictions of children even if they are clothed. This would have posed some interesting problems for executives from Coppertone to Calvin Klein.

When the Justice Department argued before the Supreme Court that a Pennsylvania man should not be prosecuted for possessing videotapes of young girls because they were clothed and not acting lasciviously, conservative opponents accused President Clinton of being soft on child pornography. Civil libertarians replied that a new, more explicit and punitive law might result in pre-emptive self-censorship by publishers and librarians who did not want to be exposed to prosecution.

Subsequent developments revealed that exposure was indeed the real issue. When the more stringent regulations were drafted, Republicans in the Senate rejected them, claiming that the current law was adequate, and "the amendments only served to provide political cover for the Administration."

Legislating Morality

As usual when politics enters the realm of legislating morality, all the potential victims of exposure here are adults. But this political skirmish was another reminder of the dangers of trying to legislate esthetic and moral standards.

It is everywhere evident that the high and pop culture of the 1990's flirts with the most forbidden of all topics, the borderline between adult and child. Phobic about "child pornography," riveted by allegations about Michael Jackson [who was accused in 1993 of molesting a teenage boy], American taste makers permit and indeed encourage what might be called child impersonation. Childhood is our major cultural fetish and, not coincidentally, our major taboo.

Baby-doll dresses are on the runways, waif models are all the rage, Calvin Klein is showing dresses designed like girlish slips for the fashionable woman. Can we really keep forgetting that fashion is all about transgression, or that children are objects of desire?

"Lolita"

When Vladimir Nabokov's "Lolita," with its precocious 12-year-old heroine, was published in the superheated 1950's, it was banned in France and parts of the United States. Notoriety was as instrumental as literary merit in its subsequent popular success. In 1956 "Baby Doll," a film made by Elia Kazan with a script by Tennessee Williams, showcased a sexy Carroll Baker in

121

the role of a child bride.

From the 50's to the 90's: Today Amy Fisher gets labeled the "Long Island Lolita" and every TV producer wants a piece of her story. In the December 1993 Vanity Fair, the Coppertone kid, her bikini bottoms tugged awry by a frisky pup (an image that made its debut in the 50's), is wittily spoofed by the photographer Annie Leibovitz: there mega-muscled rapper Marky Mark, the underwear poster boy, is being de-briefed by a German shepherd.

Art Professor Investigated for "Child Pornography"

At Wayne State University in Michigan, a janitor emptying Professor Marilyn Zimmerman's wastebasket initiated a child abuse investigation when he found a photo of her three-year-old nude child. Zimmerman, a tenured art professor and widely exhibited photographer, had discarded a proof sheet of family photos that included a picture of her daughter touching her own genitals. University police raided Zimmerman's office, seized 12 boxes of negatives, photos and other work, and sought to have criminal charges brought under the state's "child sexually abusive activity" law.

Saying she could not ignore a picture that "depicted a child exhibiting sexually explicit behavior," the director of the child abuse unit in Wayne County's Prosecutor's Office, Nancy Diehl, investigated the charges. Artists, writers, and art critics nationwide protested. The prosecutor ultimately did not press charges.

"This is an incredible violation of everything I stand for," said Zimmerman. "The innocent image of a little girl owning and enjoying her own body became the template for shameful cultural projections of sexuality."

Zimmerman is asking the University for a sabbatical and to pay the legal costs of her defense against charges brought about by their agents.

"Maximum Exposure," *Censorship News*, Issue 1, 1994.

We eroticize the look of youth, but are made nervous by sexy images of children—except when they are commercially distributed by culturally approved agents: the Hollywood film, the advertising spread, the museum exhibition.

Image of Erotic Youth

Transgression and erotic borderlines have long been powerful motives for fantasy in literature and art, as they are in advertising. Museums are filled with images of naked cherubs and mischievous putti. We read them as allegories, as stories not about children's bodies but about something else. It ought to be possible both to safeguard children from exploitation and to acknowledge the importance in both high and popular culture of images of erotic youth.

If national attention is to be focused on defining child pornography, what we need is not a hasty stitching together of legislation by officials covering their flanks but an informed conversation about the power and ubiquity of such images. It is worth remembering that the classical god of love was—perhaps for good reason—pictured as a plump and seductive child.

II

Child pornography has suddenly taken center stage in our public debate. Much of the attention has focused on the Internet, from the September 13, 1995, F.B.I. sting that netted alleged on-line pedophiles, to the Exon amendment passed by the Senate that would severely restrict not just pornography but even the use of profane language in cyberspace, to the bill introduced by Orrin Hatch that would expand the reach of child pornography laws to encompass wholly imaginary, computer-generated pictures.

Meanwhile, the federal courts are so disquieted by the dangers of child sexual abuse that since the mid-1980s they have tolerated laws that define child pornography in increasingly broad and subjective terms. The Court of Appeals for the Third Circuit has upheld an interpretation of the federal child pornography laws so expansive (it could apply to exhibition of genital areas even if they are covered by clothing) even the Solicitor General initially thought it went too far.

The government crackdown is accompanied by lurid, anguished media reports about the threat to our children. Panic over child pornography is so widespread that *Time*, swept up by the hysteria, devoted a cover story to a study, conducted by a college undergraduate, filled with dire statistics about porn online—statistics later revealed to be wildly inaccurate. But the story was introduced into the Congressional Record as proof of the growing threat.

Calvin's Kiddie-Porn

Oddly, as the press and politicians wring their hands, popular culture seems transfixed by sexy images of kids. The most shameless allusion to child pornography in the history of advertising made headlines in the summer of 1995, the aborted multimillion-dollar Calvin Klein jeans campaign, replete with what looked like a pedophile's fetish photographs and sugges-

123

tive TV voiceovers.

Calvin Klein produced the kind of photographs that policy makers have been warning us were inevitable. Some would say that in a world so perverted a major designer thinks he can sell jeans by showing kids with their legs spread, we need the harshest laws imaginable. But maybe these harsh laws are not only policing but also producing the kind of cultural impulse they seek to regulate.

In fact, Calvin's kiddie-porn campaign is only part of a larger pop-culture trend. Consider that Congress rushes to introduce more laws to control child pornography, when not that long ago fashion embraced the infantilized baby-doll look for women—complete with little-girl dresses, knee socks, Mary Janes and barrettes. Before Calvin's brush with the law, supermodel Kate Moss and her waif look bred accusations that British *Vogue* was peddling child pornography. Recall that the critical hit of summer movies in 1995 was *Kids*, with its graphic display of young teenage sexual recklessness. Think about Sally Mann, one of the art world's most successful photographers, who rose to fame taking nude portraits of her children that some people see as erotic. Rock star Courtney Love is known for her sexy, infantilized dress; gussied up like a naughty schoolgirl, her come-on is "molest me."

Perhaps these cultural phenomena suggest that as the law clamps down, it only heightens the transgressive allure of sexualized images of children. Certainly, the Calvin Klein noncampaign was a staggering success. It didn't just create media hoopla; it sold jeans. And the canceled ads have become hip collectors' items. With all the government and media focus on child pornography, it seems as if such an ad campaign was predestined, searching out and violating the hottest taboo. After all, jeans sell the image of the sexual outlaw. Like a cool teenager, Calvin said with a swagger that nothing scared him, certainly not the sexual threat that has preoccupied our policy makers. He defied authority and gained instant credibility with rebellious kids.

Sometimes pop culture responds to the law as if it were a dare. And each response, each more outrageous cultural gesture—from Calvin Klein's to Courtney Love's—only escalates the cycle, driving a legal crackdown that adds a taboo thrill to its violation. Obviously we need tough laws to protect children from pornographic exploitation. But perhaps our panic over the serious and real problem of child porn—and our expression of this panic in sweeping new laws and broader interpretations of old ones—somehow backfires. Law works by putting up boundaries, but popular culture works by locating these boundaries and tearing them down.

"We need to take reasonable steps to protect children on the information superhighway instead of simply handing the keys of our homes to pornographers."

Regulations on Internet Pornography Will Protect Children

Jim Exon

Jim Exon is the Democratic U.S. senator from Nebraska. He is the coauthor of the Communications Decency Act, which was signed into law as part of the Telecommunications Deregulation and Reform Bill of 1996. In the following viewpoint, Exon argues that the act, which applies existing obscenity laws to Internet communications, will help shield children from Internet pornography without significantly threatening the public's First Amendment rights.

As you read, consider the following questions:

1. What penalties does the Communications Decency Act impose on those who transmit pornography on networks that are accessible to children, as described by the author?
2. How does Exon respond to the charge that the Communications Decency Act threatens free speech?
3. How can children's access to the Internet be restricted, according to Exon?

Jim Exon, "Only the Force of Law Can Deter Pornographers," *Computerworld*, February 19, 1996. Reprinted by permission.

Children and families won an important victory in Congress on Feb. 1, 1996.

The Telecommunications Deregulation and Reform Bill, which includes the Exon-Coats Communications Decency Act, was passed by the Senate and House. Congress agreed that we need to take reasonable steps to protect children on the information superhighway instead of simply handing the keys of our homes to pornographers.

Rules of the Road

Some basic rules of the road are necessary to make the information superhighway safer and more useful for children and families.

Because our legislation follows previous court rulings, it won't violate the First Amendment. It makes clear that current obscenity laws apply to computers. It protects users from on-line harassment and prohibits the use of a computer to lure children into illegal sexual activity.

The legislation also provides for compliance through the good-faith use of "reasonable, effective and appropriate means" to restrict children's access to indecent or pornographic material.

The Communications Decency Act could help to ensure that our kids have a chance to travel safely through cyberspace and would still let adults access whatever legal material they choose. It would apply to computers the same antipornography laws that exist for U.S. mail, broadcast and telephone communications. The legislation focuses clearly on wrongdoers.

If someone let a child browse freely through an adult bookstore or an X-rated video arcade, I suspect and hope that most people would call the police to arrest that person. Yet these very offenses occur every day in America's electronic neighborhoods. A child can get on the information superhighway and freely ride to on-line "red light districts" that contain some of the most perverse and depraved pornographic material available.

Protecting Kids from Indecency

The Supreme Court has said repeatedly that Congress may act to protect kids from indecency.

A recent FBI sting operation resulted in the arrest of several people nationwide for distributing child pornography over computers, which shows that some of our child pornography laws also work in the world of cyberspace. But we need more legal tools to deal with this type of problem before more child victims are lured into pornography. Our law will shield children from pornography that is only a few clicks away on their computers and will make it illegal to engage children in sexual conversations on-line.

It will impose penalties on people who transmit pornographic material via computer networks that are accessible to children. The maximum penalty for such an offense would be up to two years in jail and a fine of up to $250,000.

Indecency and Free Speech

Don't let opponents of the legislation fool you: Nothing in it applies to constitutionally protected speech between consenting adults. It simply says a person can't use a computer to transmit or display indecent material in a way that is openly accessible to a person under 18 years of age.

This law will be enforced the same way as our existing pornography laws: If someone files a complaint, law enforcement will investigate. Federal privacy laws haven't been repealed. "Cybercops" won't surf the 'net to look for violators. Indecent communications simply must be conducted in a place that is out of reach for children.

Reprinted by permission: Tribune Media Services.

Access for children can be restricted in several ways, including requiring use of a verified credit card, debit account, adult access code or adult personal identification number. The Supreme Court already has approved such means for limiting child access to telephone "dial-a-porn" services.

Parents, schools and a responsible industry still must be involved in the effort to make the Internet safer. But does anyone really think that parents can monitor their children all of their waking hours? We need the added deterrent of law so that those who would pervert the network will think twice.

Our legislation has steered the industry toward developing possible blocking devices, and we applaud those efforts. Unfortunately, expensive and complicated screening devices alone don't hold enough hope of adequate success.

Opponents forsake reason when they say they want to protect children from indecency, seduction and harassment but maintain that the overriding issue is freedom of access to anything by anybody. Tell that to a parent who has had a child lured away by a deviant on a computer network. Hardly a day goes by without another story about the mix of depravity and children on the 'net. How many more are never reported?

'Net Protection

We have laws against murder, and we have laws against speeding. We still have murder, and we still having speeding. But I think most reasonable people would agree that we very likely would have more murders and more speeders if we didn't have laws as deterrents.

This measure won't make the Internet pristine, but it will help protect our children.

There is too much of the self-serving philosophy of the hands-off elite. They seem to rationalize that the framers of the Constitution plotted to make certain that the profiteering pornographer, the pervert and the pedophile be free to practice their pursuits in the presence of children on a taxpayer-created and subsidized computer network.

That is nonsense.

> *"The net may well be the first empirically lawless domain of modern life."*

Regulations on Internet Pornography Will Be Ineffective

Gary Chapman

In the following viewpoint, Gary Chapman argues that attempts to censor Internet pornography cannot be successful. He contends that the global nature of the Internet, the capacity for user anonymity, and other factors make any attempt to regulate use of the Internet unfeasible. Chapman is director of the 21st Century Project, a research and education program on science and technology policy at the University of Texas at Austin.

As you read, consider the following questions:

1. What does Chapman mean when he refers to the Internet as a "supranational entity"?
2. Why does anonymity hinder censorship of the Internet, in the author's opinion?
3. According to Chapman, why do Internet activists oppose government intervention in cyberspace?

Gary Chapman, "Net Gain," *New Republic*, July 31, 1995. Reprinted by permission of the *New Republic*; ©1995, The New Republic, Inc.

Senator James Exon of Nebraska is a grandfatherly, slow-talking, mush-mouthed poster-boy for the unwired. He admits that he had never used the Internet before somebody alerted him to the presence there of hard-core pornography. But, on June 14, 1995, the Senate passed, 84-16, Exon's amendment to the omnibus telecommunications reform bill, a legislative bomb called the Communications Decency Act of 1995. The amendment, co-sponsored by Senator Dan Coats of Indiana, outlaws "obscene, lewd, lascivious, filthy or indecent" communication on the Internet.

The response on the net itself has been explosive. Critics charge the bill is a ham-handed attempt at government regulation of a communications medium that is exemplary precisely because of its lack of regulation. Newt Gingrich has argued that it is "clearly a violation of free speech, and it's a violation of the right of adults to communicate with each other." On these grounds the bill is, indeed, troubling. But the more pressing issue is that the Internet, for technical reasons perhaps beyond the ken of Senator Exon, is largely immune not just to this but to *any* form of government regulation that net users oppose. There are already myriad ways that controversial regulations can be circumvented or foiled. In that sense the net may well be the first empirically lawless domain of modern life.

A Supranational Entity

For perhaps the first time in its history, the United States is now blanketed by a supranational entity, in which government may have little influence. It is this characteristic of cyberspace that some of its most ardent enthusiasts claim is its most portentous innovation. And, indeed, there are a number of technical features of the Internet that make this idea plausible. For example:

The Global Web. The way the Internet works makes computers halfway around the world as proximate and as useful as machines in the next room—in fact, in some cases, preferable: several Central European countries have routed nearly all their national data traffic through U.S. networks because of the capacity and speed of the U.S. connections; the Peruvian government is currently carrying on a computer war with the Shining Path guerrillas, with both sides trying to wipe out data on their respective computers in Peru, while using an Internet server in Brooklyn. UseNet news groups, where one finds most of the pornography available on the Internet, are international. Moreover, because a foreign user can send data through a U.S. computer, and U.S. users can use foreign Internet sites, it can be difficult to trace where a message originated.

Anonymity. It's easy to conceal one's identity on the Internet and hard to find the "real" person behind an electronic disguise.

An occasional contributor of pornographic pictures to a UseNet news group identifies himself as "George W. Bush," the name of the governor of Texas. No one suspects the governor of being a pornographer; but no one can determine the true identity of the person using his name by reading this guy's messages, either. In theory, you could deal with this problem by passing laws to the effect that whoever actually provides Internet access is legally responsible for the messages that originate there, but to do so would risk infuriating every single access provider and incurring lawsuits. (The original version of the Exon bill included such a provision, but the reaction from corporations, universities and private network service providers was so hostile that Exon dropped that strategy and targeted the senders instead.)

Peter Stein. Reprinted with permission.

This matter is further complicated by the existence of what are called anonymous mailers. Already a feature of the Internet, anonymous mailers are machines that one can send a message to and which will then automatically forward the message minus any clues to its original source. There is an active anonymous mailer in Finland now, for example, broadcasting messages and images around the world with no identification of their authors. FBI Director Louis Freeh wants to ban anonymous mailers, but if they're banned in the U.S., they will undoubtedly proliferate overseas.

Expansion and Coding

Overwhelming data volume. Internet traffic has been growing by between 15 and 20 percent a month—an unprecedented rate of expansion, for anything—and institutions are strained trying to keep up with demand. Terabytes, or trillions of bytes, are circulating on the net at any given time. Trying to locate illegal or offensive data on the net would be harder than trying to isolate two paired words in all the world's telephone conversations and TV transmissions at once. And this difficulty grows worse every hour.

Encryption. There is currently a struggle going on between, on the one side, government officials who want to control standards for encryption (programs used to put data into code) so that law enforcement and national security agencies can decrypt data transmissions at will and, on the other, privacy advocates who want to use private, unbreakable codes. Already encryption algorithms are available for Internet communication that allow messages to be coded at their source and then decoded only at their intended destination. Between coding and decoding, data can appear as gibberish to anyone without the correct decoding scheme. The data can even appear as something innocuous, like a popular song or a children's story, and yet conceal something illegal.

Censorship Made Impossible

All of these features of the Internet make censorship technically impossible, and the Exon bill will be unenforceable in any reasonable sense. They also make *any* government regulation of the net problematic if not ultimately futile.

The technical characteristics of the Internet are combining with net users' rising disdain for government to produce an incrementally refined resistance to regulation. Government intervention is, thus, opposed by Internet activists not because of its specific intent but because regulation represents a penetration of alien and unwelcome ideas into perhaps the only domain where rules and behavior are largely disconnected from government coercion. In cyberspace, one allegedly leaves behind politicians, bureaucrats, police, armies and not only crime but the very concept of crime. Consider, for example, this recent message from a group calling itself DigitaLiberty, a "group" that exists only in cyberspace:

> DigitaLiberty is not hopeful that widespread freedom will come to the physical world, at least not in our lifetime. Too many constituencies depend upon the largess and redistributive power of national governments and therefore oppose freedom and the individual responsibility it entails. But we do believe that liberty can and will prevail in the virtual domains we are building on the net and that national governments will be powerless to stop us. We believe that cyberspace will transcend national borders, national cultures and national economies. We believe that no one will hold sovereignty over this new realm because coercive force is impotent in cyberspace.

Much of this kind of rhetoric can be dismissed as naive and deluded, of course. Millions of network users are legitimately worried about their kids having access to pictures of bestiality and worse, and most don't tend to ponder the utopian potential of cyberspace. It's also the case that most Internet users access the net from deep within bureaucratic institutions, and it is typically these bureaucracies that profit and are strengthened most by computer networks, despite what the visionaries claim.

Cyberspace vs. Pornography

But it is also true that the so-called "digerati," as some mavens of digital culture have taken to calling themselves, are now the intellectual vanguard for an internationalist, libertarian worldview of global, amoral, stateless capitalism, and this is increasingly in conflict with the nativist, patriotic "family values" apparently ascendant in the American middle class. Eighty-six senators voted for the Exon bill, and it was an easy call for most of them. Americans are still ambivalent about cyberspace, but they know how they feel about pornography.

As the Internet and multinational corporations drift away from their national moorings, politics and morality seem to be burrowing deeper into the secure comforts of national culture. This is typically expressed in terms of national sovereignty, which is why cultural traditionalists, like Patrick Buchanan, are often zealous nationalists. But the global character of the Internet, and the culture it is engendering, challenges and weakens such parochialism, even as the Internet penetrates our homes and the computers on our office desks. And this is something that few of our politicians, including those eager to regulate cyberspace, have really begun to grasp.

"If pornography does in fact deny women equal opportunities for autonomous lives, the state can legitimately outlaw it."

Censorship of Pornography May Benefit Women

David McCabe

In the following viewpoint, David McCabe finds merit in the arguments made by radical feminists who favor censoring pornography. He concludes that if pornography encourages violence and other harms against women, as antipornography feminists insist, then censorship is a legitimate means of protecting women from such threats. McCabe is a graduate student in philosophy at Northwestern University in Evanston, Illinois.

As you read, consider the following questions:

1. What are the conservative objections to pornography, as stated by the author?
2. How does the feminist critique of pornography improve on the conservative view, in McCabe's opinion?
3. Why is it unwise to indiscriminately maximize individual liberty, according to the author?

David McCabe, "The Politics of Porn: Not-So-Strange Bedfellows," *In These Times*, March 7, 1994. Reprinted with permission.

Perhaps the sole indisputable fact about pornography is that it has occasioned a seemingly unlikely alliance between conservative Republicans and radical feminists. Commentary on this unusual coalition consists mostly of tired reflections on the strange bedfellows politics makes, with little serious analysis of the dynamics linking these groups. The general view seems to be that this alignment of forces is simply the result of an unusual set of circumstances. This interpretation is understandable; it is, after all, hard to imagine that figures like Andrea Dworkin and Jesse Helms have anything in common beyond a shared wish to see pornography disappear.

But there are deeper connections between the ideologies of the two groups. The feminist critique is less radical than it might at first appear. In some ways it offers a continuation of, and improvement on, a conservative argument many decades old.

Conservative Objections

Most conservative objections to pornography, to be sure, stem from the notion that sex is basically a messy activity, proper only for married couples, which should be neither discussed nor thought about much. But in addition to this impoverished conservatism, there is a more reasonable and potentially more powerful conservative argument, put forth by the British jurist Patrick Devlin, that merits closer attention.

Devlin's claim is that any society has a legitimate right to protect itself against threats to its structure; since part of that structure is a shared morality, whatever threatens that moral structure is a legitimate object of legislation. Society may thus outlaw behavior that deviates from its shared morality for the same reason that it may prosecute treason; in each case it is acting to protect itself. And because society is acting in self-defense "there are no theoretical limits to legislation against immorality." Any immoral action may be outlawed if society agrees that it would inspire in the "right-minded person" intolerance, indignation and disgust. Judgments in these matters, asserts Devlin, are not susceptible to logical argument; instead, they are a matter of "real feeling."

Liberals responding to Devlin have quite rightly criticized his willingness to dismiss the role of logical argument in justifying moral judgments and his enthronement of feeling as the final arbiter of society's morality. A gut "feeling" of revulsion at an activity is simply not by itself legitimate grounds to restrict that activity. The danger of Devlin's argument is that mere assertions of feeling and ungrounded assertions of distaste take the place of moral reasoning.

There are, then, two chief failings in conservative arguments against pornography: either they simply assume the value of a community's moral standards without making the case for them (as in Devlin's case), or they rely on moral standards (e.g., a puritanical approach to sexuality) that are largely unpersuasive today.

The Feminist Critique

But these failings are not insurmountable. The great promise of the feminist critique of pornography is that, unlike the conservative arguments, it makes clear both the intrinsic value of the standards violated by pornography and the damage to society caused by violating those standards.

Sexuality of Dominance and Submission

There is a close historical connection between pornography and prostitution. (The word *pornography* itself means, quite literally, "writing about prostitutes.") Along with the concern and debate over prostitution, then, an even fiercer debate is raging in the current women's movement over pornography.

The name most prominently associated with the abolitionist view regarding pornography is Catharine A. MacKinnon, professor of law at the University of Michigan Law School. In her own contribution to *Feminism and Political Theory*, entitled "Sexuality, Pornography, and Method: Pleasure Under Patriarchy," MacKinnon focuses on the processes by which the social subordination of women to men is accomplished and maintained under patriarchy—processes in which, she claims, the learning and practice of a sexuality of dominance and submission play a crucial role. To MacKinnon, pornography is one of the ways in which the system of dominance and submission is maintained, a system whose underlying dynamic depends on the sexual objectification of women. MacKinnon places the dehumanization of women along a continuum of female submission—from visual appropriation of the female in pornography, to physical appropriation in prostituted sex, to forced sex in rape, to sexual murder.

Alice Leuchtag, *The Humanist*, May/June 1995.

Central to the feminist critique is the distinction between erotica and pornography. Erotica, feminists argue, portrays sexual acts by participants who engage as equals and who are capable of equal enjoyment. Pornography, by contrast, presents women as sexual objects who exist primarily to be manipulated by men in order to satisfy male desires for domination and sexual fulfillment. On this view, the distinguishing characteristic of pornography is not its explicit sexual content but is instead, to quote the 1970 U.S. Commission on Obscenity and Pornography, "the degrading and demeaning portrayal of the role and status of the human female."

Now, the fact that pornography expresses a morally repellent attitude may be cause to dislike it, but it is not by itself a reason to ban it. Our First Amendment, after all, guarantees the liberty to express even abhorrent views. But even John Stuart Mill, close to an absolutist in his defense of free expression, allowed that when the expression of an opinion constitutes "a positive instigation to some mischievous act," such expression could be curtailed.

Feminist critics see pornography as just this kind of expression. Accordingly, they argue for restricting pornography on the grounds that it leads directly to harm against women by contributing to a social environment in which women are systematically denied equal status, and because it inspires attitudes that encourage a broad range of crimes against women.

The feminist critique thus fills the central gap in Devlin's argument: the lack of a clear explanation of why certain moral ideals deserve protection. Feminists argue that by violating the moral ideals of equal respect, equal opportunity and equal freedom, pornography leads to harm against one-half of the population.

Infringements of Liberty

Some would respond that the state ought to remain neutral with regard to all moral values and simply attempt to secure as much individual liberty as possible. But indiscriminately maximizing liberty would lead to chaos, given the conflicting claims that would inevitably arise. For this reason the state cannot avoid ranking some liberties ahead of others, and doing this requires assessing the relative value of the activities requiring these liberties.

It follows, then, that if pornography does in fact deny women equal opportunities for autonomous lives, the state can legitimately outlaw it on the grounds that the infringement of the liberties of women in a society tolerating pornography is far worse than the loss of liberty that would result if society banned it.

To be sure, there are large (and perhaps insuperable) difficulties that would plague any attempt to give legal force to the feminist critique. To name just two: studies probing the link between pornography and aggression toward women seem at this point inconclusive, and the task of codifying the distinction between erotica and pornography poses an enormous challenge. Because serious objections like these remain unresolved, it is not clear that greater restrictions against pornography would be wise. The work that remains to be done is not philosophical; it involves difficult empirical and sociological research to resolve the dilemmas above. But it is clear that the insights provided by feminism have helped to clarify a principled position from which to challenge pornography.

"Censorship always hurts women."

Censorship of Pornography Harms Women

Leanne Katz

Leanne Katz is the executive director of the National Coalition Against Censorship (NCAC). In the following viewpoint, she criticizes the views of feminists who contend that pornography should be censored in order to protect women. She contends that such an approach threatens the women's movement. The struggle for women's equality and liberation depends on free expression, Katz argues, including explicit representations of sexuality.

As you read, consider the following questions:

1. According to the author, how have antipornography feminists misused the word "pornography"?
2. How has the *Butler* decision affected free expression in Canada, according to Katz?
3. What are the central elements of the model ordinance proposed for the United States, as described by Katz?

Leanne Katz, "Censorship Too Close to Home," *SIECUS Report*, October/November 1994. Reprinted with permission.

The censorship of sexually related expression may well be the greatest threat to the American system of free speech today, and attacks on sexually related expression are certainly hampering education and the open examination of sexuality. Traditional "decency" forces have found a powerful ally in censorship advocates like writer Andrea Dworkin and law professor Catharine MacKinnon, who claim their work represents *the* feminist position on "pornography." In fact, however, feminists from all walks of life, with a wide range of perspectives, are trying to dispel the myths that women want censorship, that censorship is good for women, and that supporters of censorship speak for women.

New Words, Same Old Censorship

In the past decade, the "antipornography" arguments of Dworkin and MacKinnon have gathered an intense following among those who would decide for others which sexually oriented expression should be taboo. Dworkin, MacKinnon, and their followers claim that what they call "pornography" (including works by gay men, lesbians, and straight women) is a major cause of discrimination and violence against women, and they demand laws against it. They have drafted legislation for the suppression of sexually related expression in the United States (they continue to advocate their so-called model ordinance, which the U.S. Supreme Court declared unconstitutional in 1986), and they have campaigned for similar laws abroad—notably in Canada and Great Britain. They contend that suppression is the cure for sexism and a vast array of other ills.

Dworkin and MacKinnon have supplied old-fashioned censorship with new rhetorical ammunition. They have popularized words like "degrading" and "dehumanizing" as justifications for suppression, insisting that such words offer a different legal standard than "morality" and help to classify works that are "harmful" to women.

Their rhetoric has been adopted not only by "antipornography" feminists, by those who support legal measures against "hate speech," and by others who represent themselves as being from the political left. Powerful "morality" groups now use Dworkin and MacKinnon's words, arguments, and names in their insistence on censorship.

An Ambiguous Term

The term "pornography" is ambiguous and contestable—hence my use of quotation marks. The word is not used in U.S. law, and most legal scholars and critics consider it even vaguer than "obscenity," a legal concept long infamous for its lack of clarity. (Twenty years ago, the National Coalition Against Censorship, or NCAC, was formed out of common concern by groups and individuals about several U.S. Supreme Court decisions that greatly narrowed First Amendment protection for sexually related expression. "Obscenity" laws have since led to legal actions against owners of theaters, bookstores, and record stores; artists; clerks; and even a museum director.) "Pornography" may ordinarily be used to refer to sexually explicit words and images whose sole purpose is sexual arousal. But it also is frequently the label used to attack expression vital to women.

Throughout this century, many feminists and others have been engaged in various types of sexually related expression, including education, art, literature, political activism, literary criticism, film, historical study, sociology, law, philosophy, and music. They have represented vastly different experiences, interests, and views regarding sexuality and its expressions, including what they themselves or others may celebrate or attack as pornography or erotica. Such materials may be designed, variously, to educate, disgust, entertain, arouse, shock, inspire, and much more. Figures as diverse as Margaret Sanger, Sylvia Plath, Maya Angelou, and Holly Hughes have been attacked because of the sexually related content of their work.

Nevertheless, when Dworkin and MacKinnon are asked whether a particular example of material with sexual content would be considered "pornography"—and hence legally actionable—under their proposed definition, they mockingly call the query a "what-can-I-still-have question." They seem to think any interest in a sexually explicit work is a suspicious, dangerous, and "deviant" interest, which should be subject to an "official" review. But even the closest of friends can endlessly discuss whether a particular passage or scene dealing with sexuality is valid and has intellectual or artistic integrity, or is seriously exploitative, whether and how it is sexist, what kinds of effects it may have, and different ways it might be looked at or analyzed. But neither in writing nor in speaking do Dworkin and MacKinnon ever refer to a sexually related work that would be legally "acceptable" to them, whether as art, as literature, as education, or for sexual enjoyment.

The *Butler* Decision

In 1992, the Canadian Supreme Court provided an unusual reality test of MacKinnon and Dworkin's theories. In its decision in an obscenity case (*Donald Victor Butler v. Her Majesty the Queen*), the Court adopted arguments from a legal brief that MacKinnon wrote with two others, and upheld and reinterpreted Canada's obscenity law. The decision said that sexually explicit expression that is "degrading" or "dehumanizing" or that depicts violence is "obscene" and illegal because of the public opinion that it "harms" women. The Court found no evidence of

140

"harm," but nonetheless claimed to be acting on behalf of women and children.

Dworkin and MacKinnon say that the claim of "harm" is a different justification for censorship from arguments about "morality." They criticize "morality" as the reason for suppressing sexual expression because words like "scurrilous," "disgusting," "indecent," and "immoral," when used to define punishable expression, are sometimes taken to justify the patriarchal view "that women's naked bodies are indecent, sexual displays are immodest, unchaste and impure, homosexuality is repulsive and sex outside of traditional marriage or in other than traditional configurations is a sin." By contrast, MacKinnon suggested to the Canadian Supreme Court, words such as "dehumanizing," "degrading," and "subordinating" offer a definition that will prohibit only material that "harms" women.

Justice John Sopinka used that argument when he wrote in the *Butler* decision: "This type of material would, apparently, fail the community standards test not because it offends against morals but because it is perceived by public opinion to he harmful to society, particularly to women." He continued, quoting approvingly from another case, *Town Cinema Ltd. v. The Queen:* "'The most that can be said, I think, is that the public has concluded that exposure to material which degrades the human dimensions of life to a subhuman or merely physical dimension and thereby contributes to a process of *moral* desensitization must be harmful in some way'" (emphasis added).

MacKinnon said of *Butler:* "This makes Canada the first place in the world that says what is obscene is what harms women, not what offends our values." Dworkin commented: "Most obscenity laws are based on a hatred of women's bodies and homophobia; the Canadian law is very different."

But feminists, gay men, lesbians, and artists, among other groups, opposed the decision, and worried about how it would be used. They agreed with Thelma McCormack, director of the Canadian Centre for Feminist Research, when she said, "The *Butler* decision belongs to the Right. The Supreme Court of Canada doesn't give a damn about gender equality. It is concerned about control, and was pleased to have a feminist gloss put on it."

Who Decides?

Since *Butler*, numerous cases have illustrated the sad answer to the oft-asked question about censorship: Who decides? The Canadian government—including the police (through Project Pornography, a joint vice squad of the Toronto and Ontario police departments), Canada Customs, and the courts—has attacked, seized, threatened, fined, and banned a wide variety of feminist, gay, lesbian, and other materials and people involved with these works.

Almost immediately after *Butler*, police targeted a lesbian magazine, *Bad Attitude*; Glad Day, a small lesbian and gay bookstore in Toronto, was successfully prosecuted for carrying an issue of the magazine containing what the court ruled was a "violent," "degrading," and "dehumanizing" short story. This was the first post-*Butler* obscenity conviction. In reference to this censorship, Dworkin declared: "Lesbian porn is an expression of self-hatred. . . . When it is trafficked in the world, it becomes a social reality."

Subsequently, the *Butler* "degrading and dehumanizing" standard was used in a court case that upheld the pre-*Butler* Customs banning of several gay comic books and magazines. The court ruled that the materials were obscene, often only because they involved gay sexual behavior. Catharine MacKinnon, under intense criticism, claimed that the court applied *Butler* incorrectly. But neither court nor cop asked her opinion, and the decision stands. Who decides?

Butler has also negatively affected the case of Vancouver's Little Sisters Book and Art Emporium. This small bookstore is challenging the seizures by Customs of yet more lesbian and gay material. The store's appeal to the courts had been delayed pending the *Butler* decision, which has now seriously handicapped its legal arguments. The Little Sisters case (which has so far cost the bookstore more than $80,000 in legal fees) has been repeatedly delayed, and has yet to come to trial.

Since *Butler*, Canada Customs has detained, prohibited, and—as Customs put it—"inadvertently destroyed" a huge number and wide variety of feminist, lesbian, gay, and other works, including some by Susie Bright, Pat Califia, Kathy Acker, David Leavitt, the Marquis de Sade, Charles Bukowski, and Andrea Dworkin.

A Delicious Irony?

A certain amount of confusion has surrounded the seizures of shipments of Dworkin's books. MacKinnon has claimed that Customs officials "encountered" two books by Dworkin, and then "found to their embarrassment within about a week" that the books were not "bad." But according to notices Customs sent to the Montreal bookstore Le Dernier Mot, the agency detained shipments of Dworkin's *Woman Hating* and *Pornography: Men Possessing Women*, and officially determined them to be prohibited by the "degrading and dehumanizing" standard. Then, approximately three months after the books were shipped (and one week after the case received intense publicity), Customs released them without following any of the agency's own reevaluation procedures. Dworkin, MacKinnon, and their followers seem to believe that anticensorship feminists consider this episode nothing but a delicious irony, but they are wrong. This type of attack was inevitable, and feminists who are against censorship deeply oppose it.

Censorship crusaders claim that the widely publicized actions of Canada Customs are unrelated to their *Butler* "victory." But the Canadian Supreme Court interpreted the criminal code; Customs upholds it. Customs was already using the rhetorical and now popular "degrading and dehumanizing" standard, which Dworkin and MacKinnon say is so important and which *Butler* wrote into law. Customs and, as yet, the Canadian courts, do not deem it necessary to revise or clarify these regulations. *Butler* has encouraged Customs to step up attacks on so-called degrading and dehumanizing material. As feminist theorist Pat Califia has said: "The *Butler* decision says [to Customs] you are not prudes. You are white knights defending womanhood and preventing battery and rape."

Almost 10 percent of MacKinnon's book *Only Words* is devoted to praise for Canada's acceptance of her ideology. Yet, in the book, MacKinnon says not a word about the real-life consequences of her Pyrrhic victory. She insists that censorship is the remedy for sexism, racism, and homophobia. Among Canadian writers, readers, activists, and scholars, there is widespread anger at MacKinnon, Dworkin, and their followers. At a 1993 symposium, a lesbian speaker said of censorship campaigners: "You handed them the language they had been looking for, the 'degrading and dehumanizing' language, and now they are busting our bookstores." Well over half of Canadian feminist bookstores have had materials seized by Customs.

MacKinnon and others claim that before *Butler*, Canada's obscenity law was much easier to "abuse." But are words like "immoral" and "indecent" more flexible than words like "degrading" and "dehumanizing"?

A Thwarted Campaign in the United States

Fortunately, in the United States, this "feminist antipornography" campaign was thwarted in 1986, when the Supreme Court affirmed that the so-called civil rights censorship proposal drafted by Dworkin and MacKinnon, and passed by conservative forces in Indianapolis, violated the First Amendment. In *American Booksellers Association v. Hudnut*, the Court summarily affirmed the Seventh Circuit finding of unconstitutionality—that is, it acted without feeling the need for briefing or oral argument. In an amici curiae brief, a wide range of prominent feminists, including Betty Friedan, Kate Millett, and Adrienne Rich, told the Court they were against the ordinance. Today, many feminists—including members of the NCAC's Working Group on Women, Censorship, and "Pornography"—continue to fight to get the message out that censorship always hurts women. It is disturbing that this repressive and untenable legislation is still advocated.

Even though MacKinnon was instrumental in the Canadian *Butler* decision, and Dworkin-MacKinnonites have publicly praised and defended it, Dworkin and MacKinnon naively insist that their U.S. proposal is different. Their "model ordinance" is not an obscenity law, but it amounts to more of the same old censorship demands. Its central elements are as follows:

- another vague definition of "pornography," which begins: "the graphic sexually explicit subordination of women through words and/or pictures" and uses undefined terms like "degrading," "dehumanizing," and "harm";
- the designation of "pornography" as sex discrimination (or "harm"); and
- the provision that anyone "harmed" may bring suit against "traffickers" in "pornography."

"Trafficking" may conjure images of drugs and white slavery. But the ordinance would permit suits for civil rights violations against teachers, artists, filmmakers, writers, bookstore owners, and even book and video store clerks, among others (any of whom may be feminists), because they write, create, or make available words or images a plaintiff considers "pornography."

Well-intentioned individuals can learn from the Canadian "experiment." Most people remember, some of the time, that censorship does not only happen to books, it happens to society. Women's equality and liberation require ongoing and unorthodox conceptualization, discussion, and dissent about sexuality and its possibilities. Every disadvantaged group and individual needs the strongest possible system of free expression to voice grievances and to agitate for change. Unfortunately, it often takes a disastrous censorship movement—too close to home—to serve as a reminder of how important it is to constantly guard against those who would restrict rights of expression.

Periodical Bibliography

The following articles have been selected to supplement the diverse views presented in this chapter. Addresses are provided for periodicals not indexed in the *Readers' Guide to Periodical Literature*, the *Alternative Press Index*, the *Social Sciences Index*, or the *Index to Legal Periodicals and Books*.

Susie Bright and Susan Hayes — "Women on Women," *New Statesman & Society*, March 8, 1996.

Avedon Carol — "Free Speech and the Porn Wars," *National Forum*, Spring 1995. Available from PO Box 16000, Baton Rouge, LA 70893-1410.

Alisa L. Carse — "Pornography: An Uncivil Liberty?" *Hypatia*, Spring 1995.

Andrea Dworkin et al. — "Pornography and the New Puritans: Letters from Andrea Dworkin and Others," *New York Times Book Review*, May 3, 1992.

Joanne Furio — "Does Women's Equality Depend on What We Do About Pornography?" *Ms.*, January/February 1995.

Sarah Kershaw — "Against Pornophobia," *New York*, January 16, 1995.

Elizabeth M. Matz — "An Open Memo to Men: A Brief Reflection on Pornography Leads to a Reflective Tirade in Statistical Mode," *Women and Therapy*, Summer 1994.

Mark Nichols — "Viewers and Victims," *Maclean's*, October 11, 1993.

Glynis O'Hara — "The Boring Truth About Porn," *World Press Review*, October 1995.

Ruth Rosen — "Not Pornography," *Dissent*, Summer 1994.

Diana E.H. Russell — "Politicizing Sexual Violence: A Voice in the Wilderness," *Women and Therapy*, Winter 1995.

Jeffrey G. Sherman — "Love Speech: The Social Utility of Pornography," *Stanford Law Review*, April 1995.

Jeffrey Toobin — "X-Rated," *New Yorker*, October 3, 1994.

Chris Townsend — "A Picture of Innocence?" *History Today*, May 1996.

Should the Entertainment Media Be Censored?

CENSORSHIP

Chapter Preface

The American Psychological Association estimates that the average American child sees one hundred thousand acts of violence on TV before reaching the age of thirteen. Congress reacted to this trend in 1996 by passing a telecommunications act that, in part, requires television manufacturers to install a special computer chip—a V-chip—in every television set. The V-chip enables parents to block programs with excessive violence from showing on their televisions.

In order for the V-chip to be effective, a rating system must be developed to determine which programs are violent. Television executives have agreed to devise such a rating system. However, if the television industry is unable to create a system, the Federal Communications Commission (FCC) will institute one of its own.

Proponents of the V-chip believe the telecommunications act marks an important step in controlling violence on television. "Having a rating system, in and of itself, is going to make producers more thoughtful about the material they're presenting," states Rowell Huesmann, a professor of communication at the Institute for Social Research at the University of Michigan.

However, opponents see the V-chip requirement as a threat to rights guaranteed by the First Amendment. Critics especially fear the prospect of an FCC rating system, which they contend would put the federal government in a position to regulate the content of television broadcasting. Nick Gillespie, an assistant editor for *Reason* magazine, argues that "there's no question that the [V-chip] legislation is intended to use governmental muscle to change what people watch."

The V-chip has been criticized on the grounds that the new technology will lead to censorship of television programming. However, many Americans believe that censorship of television shows—as well as of movies, song lyrics, and other forms of entertainment media—is justified due to the increasingly violent and sexually explicit nature of these programs. Censorship of the entertainment media is the topic of the following chapter.

*"If shaming them doesn't work? There's always
the C-word waiting in the wings."*

Censorship of the Entertainment Media May Be Necessary

George R. Plagenz

In the following viewpoint, syndicated columnist George R. Plagenz describes efforts to pressure the entertainment industry into producing less offensive music and films. Plagenz contends that if these attempts fail, censorship may be necessary. He points out that from the 1920s to the 1960s, Hollywood films were censored by the Hays Office (named after Will Hays), and he argues that such an approach may be needed again if Hollywood executives refuse to voluntarily reduce the objectionable content in their products.

As you read, consider the following questions:

1. What did Bob Dole accuse Time Warner of doing, according to Plagenz?
2. According to the author, when were Hollywood's "golden years"?
3. What was "censorship's dying gasp," in the author's opinion?

George R. Plagenz, "Will Hollywood Clean Up Its Act?" Saints and Sinners column, May 24, 1996. Reprinted by permission of Newspaper Enterprise Association, Inc.

No one has mentioned censorship—yet. At this point, Hollywood's growing number of angry critics is hoping to shame the film and video producers into cleaning up their act.

Sen. Robert Dole, R-Kan., made the best attempt at it so far in a speech to the executives of the entertainment industry in May 1995. Speaking to these grown men like a high school principal dressing down a group of shiftless students who were frittering away their youth in banal pursuits, Dole said, half reproachfully, half sadly, "Is this what you intended to accomplish with your careers?" The GOP presidential candidate accused Time Warner, a giant in the music business, of trafficking in cultural trash and giving the country "nightmares of depravity." If there were any others out there "cultivating moral confusion for profit," Dole warned, "we will use their names and shame them as they deserve to be shamed."

The C-Word

And if shaming them doesn't work? There's always the C-word waiting in the wings. While Dole never mentioned the word censorship, what he said made the Hollywood bigwigs think of it all on their own. There had been, they knew, censorship once before at a time similar to this. Could those days come again?

It was the Legion of Decency, the morals watchdog of the Catholic Church, that was primarily responsible for imposing censorship on the movies. Sex on the screen and Hollywood sex scandals off the screen were destroying the film capital's image with the public. Mae West in particular was giving the bluenoses fits with her insinuating talk and walk. "Why doncha come up and see me sometime?" was her classic line. Double entendres such as "I've Found a New Way to Go to Town" were also drawing deep frowns from the Legion of Decency. In the face of such "outrage" and threatened with a boycott of Catholic moviegoers, the film bosses decided they had better police their own morals before somebody else stepped in and did it for them. They organized the Motion Picture Producers and Distributors of America and named Will Hays as their president with all the powers of a censor.

Hays had perfect credentials for the job. An elder in the Presbyterian Church, teetotaler and non-smoker who never swore, coming from small-town America (Sullivan, Ind.), Hays rose to become chairman of the Republican National Committee and, like Dole, a candidate for the GOP presidential nomination (in 1920). Warren Harding got the nod, but he later rewarded Hays for his support by naming him U.S. postmaster-general. Hays left that job a year later to take the movie post.

As movie czar from 1922 to 1945, Hays ran a "tight ship." According to Gerald Gardner's book about the Hays Office years, titled *The Censorship Papers*, even the mildest vulgarities, like a burp, were blue-penciled from a script. But protests by authors and producers that the Hays Office was ruining their creative efforts do not appear to have had much validity. Quite the contrary. The 1930s, when the studios raised the cry that they were being forced to operate under impossibly restrictive moral standards, turned out to be Hollywood's "golden years."

©Britt/Copley News Service. Reprinted with permission.

Though the Hays Office would stay afloat until 1968, by the early 1960s the once "tight ship" was taking on water and sinking rapidly. When *Who's Afraid of Virginia Woolf?* was given the censors' seal of approval in 1963 after an appeal by Warner Brothers, it was censorship's dying gasp. The Edward Albee play brought to the screen a veritable avalanche of obscenities never before heard in a movie theater. The era of clean dialogue and happy endings was over. A "fine reticence" had given way to tasteless realism.

Luckily, Hays was no longer around. He had died in 1954. He would never have understood what was happening to our culture.

"Better the rough anarchy of the free market than government, directly or indirectly, telling us what we can hear and watch."

The Entertainment Media Should Not Be Censored

Mortimer B. Zuckerman

Mortimer B. Zuckerman is chairman and editor in chief of *U.S. News & World Report.* In the following viewpoint, Zuckerman concedes that the offerings of the entertainment industry—including rap music, Hollywood movies, and television shows—are increasingly violent and sexually explicit. However, he argues that the content of these products should not be censored. He insists that in order to ensure absolute freedom of speech, society must tolerate the relatively small number of offensive creations offered by the entertainment industry.

As you read, consider the following questions:

1. According to the American Psychological Association, cited by the author, how many acts of television violence does a typical child see?
2. What positive values do many Hollywood films portray, in Zuckerman's opinion?
3. What does Zuckerman say are the principal causes of violence?

Mortimer B. Zuckerman, "Forest Gump vs. Ice-T," *U.S. News & World Report*, July 24, 1995. Copyright 1995, U.S. News & World Report. Reprinted with permission.

The cultural silent majority in America is up in arms over the rising levels of violence and prurient images that have seeped into popular entertainment. Gangsta rap is the lightning rod. Popular music for the young has always been in some conflict with middle-class attitudes: When you were a teenager did 50-year-old people ever like the same music you did? But that consoling thought does not last long when you listen to the extreme preoccupation with sex and violence of an Ice-T or the Geto Boys. It seems the sociopaths are taking over music beamed at our most vulnerable group—the children.

Hollywood, the country's TV and film factory, is another focal point of public concern. It has long been the mirror of our culture and the creator of many of our national myths and heroes. Once filmmakers used to evoke sexual longings through eye contact or a touch of the elbow. Today they resort to startlingly graphic ways of presenting sex and violence. A recent poll indicates that sexual moderation and fidelity are the norm, both for married people and for those who live together. But on so-called dramatic television, 7 out of 8 sexual encounters involve extra-marital sex.

This might not be quite so bothersome if the kids weren't listening and watching. But they are: Children spend more time watching television than they do attending school. According to the American Psychological Association, a typical child sees 8,000 murders and 100,000 acts of violence on TV before graduating from elementary school. Working parents plainly worry about their inability to monitor their youngsters' viewing habits—and most would welcome President Clinton's proposal to mandate a V-chip (V for violence) that can be inserted into TV sets to program out certain shows and channels. [The V-chip proposal was passed as part of the telecommunications bill of 1996.]

The Need to Keep Cool

For all the concern, we need to keep our cool. The jury is still out on how all that TV violence affects kids in the real world. And many of the 400 or so films that Hollywood produces every year actually convey traditional virtues and mainstream verities—love, loyalty, honor, duty and compassion. Just consider *Forrest Gump*, *Little Women*, *Black Beauty*, *The Lion King* and *The Flintstones*. Even the heavily criticized *Natural Born Killers* was intended to caricature the intersection of violence and media attention in our culture. Hollywood, which has had many movies that have exposed prejudice, racism and other social problems, also maintains a rating system that informs parents which movies are unsuitable for children.

In the democracy of the marketplace, where individuals make decisions about what they will buy, read or see, some choices will veer toward the vulgar, the profane and the excessive. Americans have some sense of this. They may be irritated, or outraged, by pop culture, but the polls tell us they understand that the principal causes of violence and other national problems lie elsewhere than in the entertainment industry. They are all too aware that children are more affected by the general decline of public morality, the lack of religion, the deterioration of public schools, family breakdown and poor parenting. They could also point to a culture that emphasizes the individual over the group and that elevates self-expression to a religion. Typical is the Nike ad in which Andre Agassi and Wimbledon champ Pete Sampras stop traffic to play tennis in the middle of a busy street, then hit tennis balls at a bus that follows its route through the made-up tennis court. The tag line is "Just Do It!" Translation: Pursue your own fun despite the rules and the inconvenience to others.

The Good Will Win Out

Belief in the value of free expression is not so much rational as religious, a matter of faith. We First Amendment zealots believe that a free society demands a free marketplace of ideas where the good can compete against the bad and the ugly and that, given such a marketplace, the good will win out.

Donald Kaul, *Liberal Opinion Week*, March 28, 1994.

The price we pay for our cultural freedom is that a few noxious weeds may thrive amid the thousand flowers that bloom. Better the rough anarchy of the free market than government, directly or indirectly, telling us what we can hear and watch. We can and should fight bad speech with good speech. We can and should encourage corporate executives to think twice before putting trash on the marketplace. We can and should support those institutions that offset some of the ills of the marketplace—public television and public radio. Our culture would be infinitely poorer without them. And we should beware of politicians who would cripple or destroy these institutions while they exploit popular discomfort with mass entertainment. They must not be allowed to divert attention from the real issues facing America.

*"The only honest answer, sadly, is censorship—
the application of deliberate pressure against this
choking culture of violence."*

Violence in the Media Should Be Censored

Sidney Callahan and Bryan Appleyard

In the following two-part viewpoint, Sidney Callahan and Bryan Appleyard argue that violence in films and on television should be censored. In Part I, Callahan contends that censorship of violence is justified because people imitate the violent acts they see portrayed in the media. In Part II, Appleyard insists that censorship is the only means of ridding the popular culture of excessively violent films that possess little artistic value and that incite violence. Callahan is a columnist for *Commonweal,* an independent Catholic magazine. Appleyard writes for the *Independent,* a London newspaper.

As you read, consider the following questions:

1. What two lessons are learned by viewers of violent images, according to Callahan?
2. What does Callahan consider "our only hope"?
3. Why are violent movies made, in Appleyard's opinion?

Excerpted from Sidney Callahan, "What We See, We Do," *Commonweal,* January 12, 1996. Reprinted with permission. Bryan Appleyard, "Curbing a Culture of Violence," *World Press Review,* March 1994. Reprinted by permission of the London *Independent.*

I

Monkey see, monkey do, correct? The fire-setting and burning of a subway token-booth clerk in New York City replicates in real life a movie incident in an action thriller. Scores of such copycat crimes are regularly reported.

Violent images on TV or in the movies have inspired people to set spouses on fire in their beds, lie down in the middle of highways, extort money by placing bombs in airplanes, rape people in particularly disgusting ways, and who knows how many other kinds of shootings and assaults.

Can anyone still honestly doubt that violent and criminal images in the media or in music incite aggressive behavior? Only those making mints of money purveying violence to the great American public even try to defend the practice.

Granted, some civil libertarians who are worried about the dangers of censorship will admit we have a problem, but stoutly maintain that the price of curbing "free expression" is too high. In another part of the forest, similar arguments go on among feminists about the effects of pornography.

Defenders of the sorry state of our media will usually claim that (1) real life is violent, so why not be honest and show it; and (2) only a few vulnerable aggression-prone persons will be negatively affected, so why keep everyone else from the innocent entertainment of having a few thrills—whether of an aggressive or sexual nature. Is it the media's fault if unhinged people get set off on some rampage by what they watch or hear?

Imitation

Most psychologists who have studied the question of how aggression operates are convinced that everyone learns violent behavior by seeing it enacted, ready or not. Children will beat Bobo dolls into the ground if they have seen grown-ups do it first, and even those children who do not immediately enact the aggression learn the behavior and remember how it's done.

The more prestigious the person modeling aggressive behavior, the more likely it is to be imitated by observers. Imitation, after all, is an indispensable way that an intelligent species like ours learns.

Children do it. Teen-agers do it. Grown-ups do it. Mindlessly we automatically imitate and follow the leader. Fads sweep societies—from slang to games to foods to clothing to intellectual paradigms (and the use of words like "paradigm"). Who hasn't found herself repeating phrases recently heard? Or humming mindless TV commercials? Athletes will watch videos depicting images of excellent moves to increase their own proficiency.

Anything we notice and process gets put into the information programs in our minds and memories. When the input (horrible word but highly infectious), consists of a violent or sexually shocking act, two lessons are learned at once. One is the behavioral sequence, how, for instance, to go about setting fire to a vagrant sleeping on a park bench. The second lesson is more subtle: one learns that this kind of behavior exists; it can happen here; and it is permitted in the universe as we know it. There's the act and then there's the permission to do the unthinkable. Taboos lose their inhibitory force. And if good guys are doing horrible things in order to fight the bad guys, then the behavior is all the more permissible. Homicide rates increase in a country after its wars, whether it's a "just" or "unjust" war.

Willing to Risk Censorship

So what to do when your culture is being corrupted and poisoned? . . .

At this point I am willing to risk the dangers of censorship because I'm absolutely convinced that what you put into the imagination creates the person. Saint Paul writes to the Christians at Philippi, "Whatever is true, whatever is honorable, whatever is just, whatever is pure, whatever is pleasing, whatever is commendable, if there is any excellence, and if there is anything worthy of praise, think about these things."

What we pay attention to, becomes us, as surely as we become what we eat. Good images and good thoughts and benevolent feelings become good deeds. And alas, the opposite is also true. Maybe even truer since we may have a built-in tendency to regress into infantile rages and paranoid anxieties. And why the human fascination with blood, gore, and violence in the first place? Saint Augustine noted sadly how eagerly people were drawn to view mangled corpses, and how easily his noble and good friend Alypius was first persuaded by peer pressure to go to the Coliseum and once there, became addicted to the murderous displays of gladiatorial combat. These "games" were the thrilling entertainments of that pagan culture.

When we are bombarded continually with images of violence, brutality, sexual immorality, and betrayals of trust, our minds and spirits suffer. As the brainy heroine of Norman Rush's great novel *Mating* puts it: "The conviction that the world is secretly corrupt is dangerous to certain temperaments because it rationalizes cutting corners and being selfish, an impulse I was not in need of." And who is?

Our only hope may be in the fact that altruism is also innate and can also be imitated easily. Heroic rescuers just plunge into action without a second thought. Often they don't even want to accept praise or reward afterward because their altruistic behavior seemed to them "the only thing to do." Of course, their sense of what was "obviously necessary" had been nourished by countless prior acts of attention and good behavior. So modest altruists do deserve their medals.

Well now, thinking of all these things, what's to be done?

II

"Would you," asked Mervyn Griffith-Jones during the trial of *Lady Chatterley's Lover* in 1960, "allow your wife or your servant to read this book?" How we laughed—and still laugh—at that ponderous silliness! Yet we did not laugh when the presiding justice said at the November 1993 conclusion of the James Bulger murder trial: "It isn't for me to pass judgment on [the murderers'] upbringing, but I suspect that exposure to violent video films may, in part, be an explanation." [Two eleven-year-old boys were convicted of abducting and murdering Bulger, a two-year-old boy, in Liverpool, England.]

Convincing Evidence

A summary of over 200 studies published in 1990 . . . offers convincing evidence that the observation of violence, as seen in standard everyday television entertainment, does affect the aggressive behavior of the viewer. All types of aggressive behavior, including illegal behaviors and criminal violence, demonstrated highly significant effects associated with the exposure to television violence. The behaviors affected by viewing television violence are cause for social concern.

Leonard D. Eron, *Media & Values*, Summer 1993.

The issue of censorship connects the two cases—the issue of who, if anybody, permits or bans and whom we wish to protect. Ever since the battle [in Britain] in the 1950s to free the theater from the grip of the lord chamberlain, it has been assumed that most forms of censorship should be overthrown in the name of a morality of individual choice. Maybe there was a case for protecting children, but there could be no case for denying adults their pleasures.

This anti-censorship view was largely driven by esthetics. Modern art from French poet Charles Baudelaire to English painter Francis Bacon had dealt with the extremes of human experience. In our day, it seemed that if we were to have great art, we could not also have censors. The absolute freedom of the artist to pursue his vision wherever it might lead was to be celebrated as the primary attribute of the civilized, secular society.

This esthetic argument was made more respectably political by the insistence that it was, in some sense, the task of art to shock and disturb, or perhaps simply to reflect the underlying violence and extremity of the modern world. This obligation-to-shock argument is infantile but generally harmless in that it is only of significance in the narrow world of high art. We may not particularly admire a gruesome Robert Mapplethorpe photograph of some sadomasochistic rite, but we are unlikely to conclude that a picture exhibited in a Mayfair gallery leads to truancy and violence in Liverpool.

High Art and Splatter Movies

But the freedom of the artist to shock is also expressed in every cinema and video shop and through every satellite receiver. Film is the medium that transforms and intensifies the argument as the most esthetically dynamic and popular of modern art forms. Through cinema, the masses consume both the high art of Martin Scorsese and Francis Ford Coppola and the thousands of splatter movies now filling satellite-TV schedules and video stores.

This cinematic coexistence of the worst and the best is made even more painful by the fact that the best often looks suspiciously like the worst. Scorsese's *GoodFellas*, *Mean Streets*, and *Taxi Driver* are wonderful films that are full of the most appalling violence. The critical and popular triumph of such films confirms the industry view that violence and the movies form some kind of natural partnership.

Indeed, violence might now be said to be the primary expressive convention of the cinema. In the early 1970s, the violence of Sam Peckinpah's *Straw Dogs* made people fear for the future of the cinema. Now *Basic Instinct*, a numbing, nihilistic, unspeakably violent hymn of hate directed at all women, is blithely sold for $16.50 at the super-respectable W.H. Smith [bookstores in Europe]. Certainly, films are still censored, but the censors' lines have shifted so much and the prevalence of film violence is such that we are now in a movie world that does not feel censored at all.

The point that now has to be faced is that if you win the censorship battle—either by outright victory, as in the theater, or by stealth, as in the movies—you don't just get Mapplethorpe for the connoisseur: You get vicious drivel for the masses. More painfully, you also get unarguably fine films, such as *Taxi Driver*, *GoodFellas*, and American director Quentin Tarantino's *Reservoir Dogs*, that you would rather were not watched by the criminal classes or the mentally unstable—or by inadequately supervised children with little else in their lives.

There is a smart but easy way of dealing with this while avoiding paternalism and keeping your esthetic credentials intact. These films, you might say, are but products of the culture, evidence of deep cultural malaise.

But this is, of course, an absurd cop-out. These films are not passive expressions of culture—they are deliberately made to exploit, stimulate, and nurture a taste for blood. Other films could be made but are not because the convention of violence now exercises such a grip on both the best and the worst film-makers. We are kidding ourselves if we think that only by loosening the bonds of censorship can we have an artist of the caliber of Scorsese.

The only honest answer, sadly, is censorship—the application of deliberate pressure against this choking culture of violence. It may not work—the global media explosion will probably ensure that people can get whatever they want—but lying supine before the bloody technological invasion is not a serious alternative. It isn't freedom, either.

"A lot of people [have] stopped believing in the old and uniquely American ideal of freedom of speech."

Violence in the Media Should Not Be Censored

Patrick D. Maines

In the following viewpoint, Patrick D. Maines objects to congressional attempts to pressure television executives into reducing the violence in their programming. According to Maines, efforts to censor television violence are a first step toward widespread restrictions on the public's First Amendment rights. Maines is president of the Media Institute, a research organization that specializes in communications policy and First Amendment issues.

As you read, consider the following questions:

1. According to the author, how have journalists responded to congressional pressure to limit television violence?
2. Why is free speech no longer considered an absolute value, according to Maines?
3. Why have some free speech advocates become timid, in the author's opinion?

Patrick D. Maines, "Whatever Happened to Free Speech?" *American Journalism Review*, November 1993. Reprinted with permission.

Almost overnight, it seems, we have reached a point in our national life in which a critical mass of this country's most politically influential people accept the idea that government ought to control all manner of speech—particularly that which they fear or disfavor.

Nowhere is this more obvious than in the current firestorm over television violence. Congressional leaders, prodded by television critics and anti-violence activists, have coerced a "voluntary" agreement with the television networks to issue parental advisories on entertainment programs with violent content.

Given the fact that broadcasters traffic in the scarce and "publicly owned" electromagnetic spectrum, the industry has always been subject to more regulation than the print media. Rarely, however, have the regulations been so content-oriented and, indeed, content-specific.

Acting Out of Fear

There is little doubt the networks acted out of fear of even more regulation. As Sen. Howard Metzenbaum (D-Ohio) threatened during the Senate Constitution subcommittee's May 21, 1993, hearing on television violence, the television industry doesn't "own the airwaves . . . they have a franchise. What Congress giveth, it can taketh away."

What should be the universally appalling aspect of such a spectacle is that the parental advisories are but the beginning of broad-based content controls over once free and independent speech.

No Flood of Outrage

There has been little mention of this, however, in the media. The hearings on television violence were among the most explicitly speech-repressive events ever conducted in the halls of Congress. Yet most writers and columnists saw little cause for alarm.

Where was the flood of outrage, in the form of editorials, feature stories, op-ed pieces and syndicated columns, from journalists worried that Congress' heavy-handed coercion of the networks was an assault on the First Amendment? Reporters didn't seem to care.

Joe Urschel of *USA Today* referred to "network executives . . . squawking about victimization" and the "sanctimonious bleatings of TV's creative community." Walter Goodman wrote in the *New York Times:* "Cynicism does come easily regarding the conversion of the network brass. . . . They still had their eye on the bottom line."

Newsweek, which was intrigued by the "downcast eyes and somber expressions" of the network heads, was on the side of

Congress: "In adopting parental advisories, the networks have taken a modest first step—when what may be needed is a giant leap."

Op-ed editors weren't any more sympathetic. The *Washington Post's Sunday Outlook* section trotted out a former NBC executive who claimed to have been there 35 years ago when the order first came down to make programs more violent. And the *Wall Street Journal* offered up former Federal Communications Commission Chairman Newton Minow, who found a frighteningly eloquent way of advocating speech limits: "It is time we used the First Amendment to protect and nurture our children, rather than as an excuse to ignore them."

The Real Problem

We need to resist the censorship argument because it is so likely to backfire. No matter how much we deplore the sleaze and gore, we must keep a clear head about how they are used. Sleaze and gore are, after all, sometimes the most effective agents of consciousness-raising. It all depends on the nature of the work being considered. Films like *GoodFellas* or *River's Edge*, which depict wholly amoral, sociopathic acts of murder, are, in fact, attacks on the social realities supporting and encouraging violence. . . .

The problem, after all, is not media violence but real violence. We need to focus on the causes and the nature of that phenomenon.

Elayne Rapping, *Media & Values*, Fall 1993.

The media's lapse suggests that journalists are unaware of where their interests lie. After all, if it is permissible for government to intrude into the content of television entertainment, why not allow intrusion into television news as well? The First Amendment makes no distinction between the two.

Meanwhile, not one of the antitelevision violence organizations has had a kind word for the advisories. Instead, they are calling for much tougher restrictions; the heads of two organizations have expressed disappointment that the advisories do not cover programs with "sexual content and strong language."

Intruding on Free Speech Everywhere

If one could be assured that Congress would limit its intrusion into television programming just to the violence advisories, and if the advisories were the only example of government intrusion on free speech, one could dismiss the whole affair. Unfortunately, neither supposition is true. Congress is already moving beyond the parental advisories, and government intrudes on free speech everywhere.

Rep. Edward Markey (D-Mass.), chairman of the House Subcommittee on Telecommunications and Finance, has introduced legislation requiring all television sets to be equipped with a so-called "V-chip." When activated, this chip would block out all programming carrying a "violence" rating. [The V-chip bill was passed as part of the Telecommunications Competition and Deregulation Act in February 1996.]

In addition, Sen. Ernest Hollings (D-S.C.) has introduced a bill that would prohibit the airing of violent broadcasts during times when children are likely to be watching. Rep. John Bryant (D-Texas) has introduced legislation requiring the FCC to consider broadcasters' attempts to reduce television violence when renewing licenses. Bryant's bill would also allow the FCC to create and enforce violence standards.

Government Intrusions

As for government's intrusion into free speech generally, consider:

• By most accounts, Congress will resurrect the so-called Fairness Doctrine. The doctrine was rescinded in 1987 based on FCC findings that it chilled the coverage of controversial issues, and was likely unconstitutional under the First Amendment.

• Led by a zealous commissioner and prodded by activists, the Food and Drug Administration has begun a widespread crackdown on the promotional and educational speech of drug companies. The FDA has ruled that a drug company may not give doctors an independently published and peer-reviewed medical textbook because it mentions off-label uses (not disclosed in package inserts) for the company's products. Though commercial speech is accorded less First Amendment protection than core speech, it's no easy feat to equate a medical textbook published by a major book publisher with, say, pharmaceutical ads.

• The FDA has also issued notice of its authority over drug company video news releases. In a 1991 letter, the FDA said that video news releases should be submitted to the agency for review at the time they are initially disseminated.

• In 1990, Congress passed the Children's Television Act. This act requires television stations, as a condition of their license renewal, to provide programming that serves "the educational and informational needs of children." This explicit governmental control of program content diminishes editorial discretion in two ways: by requiring broadcasters to produce a particular category of programming, and, ipso facto, by requiring them to drop programming they would have otherwise aired.

• With the encouragement of environmental activists, in 1990 the California legislature enacted a bill making it unlawful for manufacturers to make true environmental claims about their products unless those products' environmental attributes meet certain vague and arbitrary definitions established by the legislature.

A Uniquely American Ideal

All of these attacks on free speech have a number of things in common. All are either happening now, or have happened within recent years. All have come about with the encouragement of "activist" or "special interest" groups. And finally, while all do real and direct damage to free expression, they do very little, if anything, to cure the underlying problems they are said to address.

Does anyone really believe, for instance, that portrayals of violence in television programs are even remotely as much to blame for violence in society as broken homes? Or chronic poverty? Or a legal system which does not provide for the sure and swift incarceration of hard-core criminals?

Sometime within the past few years, a lot of people stopped believing in the old and uniquely American ideal of freedom of speech—of speech that is constitutionally guaranteed against any government restrictions.

There has always been a certain amount of government regulation in order to ensure broadcasters are serving the public interest. The question now is whether it's gone too far, particularly given the number and variety of television programming options.

Prioritizing Values

How did we go from "Congress shall make no law . . ." to a society in which various interest groups advance their causes by lobbying Congress for all manner of speech restrictions?

The answer is values. Historically, freedom of speech has been regarded as the cornerstone of democracy and accorded a privileged status—guaranteed by the Constitution—as an absolute value.

Now, however, free speech has become just another worthy goal to be balanced against other worthy goals. When free speech conflicts with another value—child welfare or public health, for example—speech is often the loser.

The subhead of a *Washington Post* feature by Megan Rosenfeld summed up one journalist's attitude: "Forget the First Amendment. When It Comes to TV Violence, All I Care About Is Protecting My Kids."

But it is freedom of expression that makes the pursuit of all other political and social values possible. Clearly the Founding Fathers regarded speech as worthy of special consideration. Nevertheless, the values-balancing continues as every special interest tries to hold its values above the First Amendment.

Many liberal and broad-minded people seem to think that if things get too out of kilter the Supreme Court will set things right. Don't bet on it.

The court's First Amendment jurisprudence is more porous than is generally recognized. The court has wavered between treating free speech as an absolute value and just another social goal to be balanced and traded off.

A majority of the current court expresses its "conservatism" by deferring to legislative bodies. Moreover, as shown in the parental advisories, it is now possible for Congress merely to threaten in order to win a "voluntary" agreement which is not actionable in *any* court.

Liberal Censors

Even liberals are becoming unreliable supporters of free speech. In the past, conservatives were rightly criticized for their disregard of First Amendment freedoms. When one spoke of censorship, the censors were conservatives—setting up local censorship boards for movie theaters, banning books from school libraries, heading up crusades to outlaw adult entertainment, and so on.

Yet recently those calling for speech restrictions have come mostly from the liberal side. Certainly the Rev. Donald Wildmons of the world are still out there, but the leaders in this latest round of speech restrictions have been staunch liberals like Sens. Metzenbaum and Paul Simon (D-Ill.) and Rep. Markey.

Some blame must also rest with those of us who consider ourselves defenders of free speech. If one were to assemble two groups—special interest activists and free speech advocates—which do you think would be the larger? Which would be the fiercer and more determined?

Apologizing for Free Speech

Some First Amendment advocates have become timid and even apologetic for defending speech rights. After all, what is one little restriction compared to the health and safety of children, and many other social concerns?

The answer is that one restriction is only the beginning—and the beginning is long past us. Every blow to the First Amendment weakens it and leaves supporters less able to defend it from the next blow—and the next.

We must embrace anew the concept that speech is a unique commodity in our democracy. Ultimately we will be closer to solving the problems of society, not when we have regulated speech about every unpleasant topic, but when we allow speech to be used freely to discuss, to persuade, to precipitate change.

"The V chip will be welcomed by many parents who despair of monitoring the multitude of TV programs available to their kids."

The V-Chip
May Counteract
Television Violence

Richard Zoglin

In the following viewpoint, Richard Zoglin reports on a study that concludes that television violence is more widespread than is often believed and that a link clearly exists between television violence and aggressive behavior. Zoglin writes that the V-chip—a device that allows parents to block objectionable programming from their televisions—may help parents protect their children from the harmful effects of television violence. Zoglin is a senior writer for *Time* magazine.

As you read, consider the following questions:

1. What industry does Robert Coles compare the television industry to?
2. What findings did the National Television Violence Study make regarding the way violence is presented?
3. On what basis does Edward Markey criticize cartoons?

Excerpted from Richard Zoglin, "Chips Ahoy," *Time*, February 19, 1996; ©1996 Time Inc. Reprinted by permission.

On NBC's *Law & Order* one week, a white racist set off a bomb that killed 20 people on a New York City subway train. Tori Spelling, in the CBS movie *Co-Ed Call Girl*, grabbed a gun and shot a sleazy pimp. Batman (the cartoon character) was almost thrown into a vat of flames by the Penguin. Lemuel Gulliver (the Ted Danson character) battled gigantic bees in the land of Brobdingnag. And Nick Nolte and Eddie Murphy slapped around bad guys in the umpteenth cable showing of *48 HRS*.

It was, in other words, a pretty typical week of TV in mid-'90s America. Another week, in the view of troubled parents and concerned politicians, in which TV continued to assault youngsters with violent images, encouraging aggressive behavior in a culture where handguns and street violence are rampant. But it was also a landmark week that brought new hope to many parents worried that scenes like the above are doing untold damage to their kids.

As President Clinton signed into law the sweeping telecommunications bill passed by Congress, he officially launched the era of the V chip. A little device that will be required equipment in most new TV sets within two years, the V chip allows parents to automatically block out programs that have been labeled (by whom remains to be seen) as high in violence, sex or other objectionable material. Last week also saw the release of a weighty academic study that said, in effect, it's about time. Financed by the cable industry and conducted by four universities, the study concluded that violence on TV is more prevalent and more pernicious than most people had imagined. Of nearly 2,700 shows analyzed in a 20-week survey of 23 channels, more than half—57%—were said to contain at least some violence. And much of it was the kind that, according to the study, can desensitize kids and encourage imitation: violence divorced from the bad consequences it has in real life.

The study drew an outcry from network executives, who argued, with some justification, that they have reduced the amount of violence they air and have added warning labels for the little that remains. Indeed, a UCLA study (financed by the networks) last year found "promising signs" that levels of network violence are declining. And upon closer scrutiny, the new study's methodology does seem to overstate the case a bit. Nevertheless, it pins some hard numbers on a problem that is popping up increasingly in the public forum: What effect is TV violence having on kids? And what should we do about it?

Politicians of all stripes have jumped in. Democratic Senator Paul Simon has held well-publicized hearings on TV violence and first proposed that networks sponsor independent audits like last week's report. Bob Dole last year called for action against violence on TV as well as in movies and rock music. Democratic

Senator Joseph Lieberman of Connecticut last week joined the conservative Media Research Center in urging the networks to clean up the so-called family hour, the first hour of prime time each evening. President Clinton and Vice President Gore have both embraced the V chip and called for a summit meeting on TV violence with top network and cable executives at the end of February. The antinetwork rhetoric from many reformers sounds strikingly like that directed against another industry charged with making a harmful product. "The TV industry has to be socially responsible," says Harvard child psychiatrist Dr. Robert Coles. "We're now going after the tobacco companies and saying, 'Don't poison people.' It seems to me, the minds of children are being poisoned all the time by the networks. I don't think it's a false analogy."

The analogy depends, of course, on accepting the proposition that TV has a harmful effect on young viewers. Researchers have been sparring over that question for years, but the debate seems to have swung in favor of the antiviolence forces. The study released last week did no original research on the effect TV violence has on children's behavior. But it summarized a growing body of research and concluded that the link between TV violence and aggressive behavior is no longer in doubt. . . .

Empowering Parents

President Bill Clinton was correct when he said that the issue of V-chip technology "is not censorship; this is parental responsibility.". . .

The V-chip in no way would prevent the entertainment industry from continuing to produce whatever TV programming it deemed fit. . . . The only thing that would change is that parents concerned about what their children watch would be empowered to block out programming they find objectionable.

San Diego Union-Tribune, July 13, 1995.

The current V-chip technology, developed by a Canadian engineer named Tim Collings, is essentially a computer chip that, when installed in TV sets (added cost: as little as $1), can receive encoded information about each show. Parents can then program the TV set to block out shows that have been coded to indicate, say, high levels of violence. If, after the kids have gone to bed, parents want to watch Tori Spelling on a shooting spree, they can reverse the blocking by pushing one or more buttons.

The V chip will be welcomed by many parents who despair of

monitoring the multitude of TV programs available to their kids. The device has already been a godsend for politicians—a way of seeming to take action on TV violence while avoiding sticky issues of censorship or government control. Most children's activists welcome the device, yet recognize it is not a panacea. "The V chip doesn't do anything to decrease violence," says Arnold Fege of the National Parent-Teacher Association. "There are parents who are not going to use it at all. But it does give parents some control."

Widespread use of the V chip is probably years off. New TV sets are not required to have them for at least two years (legal challenges from the networks are expected to extend that further), and there are still all those chipless RCAs and Sonys currently in people's living rooms. Every set in the house would have to have the V chip, or else kids could just go into the bedroom to watch forbidden shows. Some critics warn, moreover, that it's only a matter of time before kids learn how to break the code and counteract the blocking mechanism.

There is another possible scenario. If the networks and advertisers learn to live with a V rating, producers might find themselves liberated—able to produce even more adult fare, secure in the knowledge that children will be shielded from it. Which could, of course, lead either to more sophisticated adult fare or sleazier entertainment. Says *Law & Order* creator Dick Wolf: "If all these shows have warnings on them, you could have a situation where producers are saying to standards people at the networks, 'I've got a warning. I can say whatever I want. I can kill as many people as I want.' "

They're already killing a lot, if the National Television Violence Study is to be believed. Billed as the "most thorough scientific survey of violence on television ever undertaken," the study not only found a surprisingly high percentage of violent shows; it also made some damning observations about the way violence is presented. According to the survey, 47% of the violent acts shown resulted in no observable harm to the victim; only 16% of violent shows contained a message about the long-term negative repercussions of violence; and in a whopping 73% of all violent scenes, the perpetrator went unpunished. These figures, however, were based on some overly strict guidelines: perpetrators of violence, for example, must be punished in *the same scene* as the violent act. By that measure, most of Shakespeare's tragedies would be frowned on; Macbeth, after all, doesn't get his comeuppance until the end of the play.

The study found significant variations in the amount of violence across the dial. On network stations, 44% of the shows contained at least some violence, vs. 59% on basic cable and 85% on premium channels like HBO and Showtime. Yet it was the broadcast networks that squawked the loudest. "Someone would have to have a lobotomy to believe that 44% of the programs on network television are violent," exclaims Don Ohlmeyer, NBC West Coast president. (Actually, the study referred to network stations, meaning that syndicated shows like *Hard Copy* were also included.) "Since I've been here, I can't think of a program we've had that's glorified violence, that hasn't shown the pain of violence and attempted to show there are other ways to resolve conflicts."

The researchers' definition of violence did, at least, avoid some of the absurdities of previous studies, in which every comic pratfall was counted. Violent acts were defined as those physical acts intended to cause harm to another; also included were verbal threats of physical harm as well as scenes showing the aftermath of violence. Thus, finding a body in a pool of blood on *NYPD Blue* counts as a violent act; Kramer bumping into a door on *Seinfeld* does not. A cartoon character whacking another with a mallet counts; but the accidental buffoonery of *America's Funniest Home Videos* doesn't.

Yet just one of these acts was enough to classify a program as violent. In addition, the survey covered a number of cable channels—among them USA, AMC, TNT, HBO and Showtime—whose schedules are filled with network reruns (including many action shows like *Starsky and Hutch* and *Kung Fu*) or theatrical films. This served to boost the overall totals of violent shows while masking the fact that violence in the most watched time periods—network prime time—has declined.

"We didn't want to get into a show-by-show debate," says Ed Donnerstein, communications and psychology professor at the University of California at Santa Barbara, where most of the monitoring was done. "We didn't want to point fingers." George Gerbner, former dean of the University of Pennsylvania's Annenberg School for Communication and a longtime chronicler of TV violence, agrees with the study's big-picture approach. "Anytime you give a name of a program, it lends itself to endless quibbling," he says. "The question is not what any one program does or doesn't do. The question is, What is it that large communities absorb over long periods of time?"

Whatever its defects, the study could have a major impact as development of the V chip begins. "This is the foundation of any rating system that will be developed," says Representative Edward Markey of Massachusetts, the V chip's original champion in Congress. The irony is that some of the most objectionable shows, in the survey's view, are cartoons and other children's shows: they are the ones that portray violence "unrealistically," without consequences or punishment. "When you show a young kid somebody being run over and they pop back up without harm, that's a problem," says Donnerstein.

"This definitely opens the door to control of TV programming by the federal bureaucracy."

The V-Chip Will Result in Censorship

Adam Thierer and Stephen Chapman

The V-chip is a device that is installed in a television set to block out programming deemed inappropriate for children. In the following two-part viewpoint, Adam Thierer and Stephen Chapman argue against a law that requires television manufacturers to install a V-chip in all new televisions and that calls for the creation of a rating system for television broadcasts. In Part I, Thierer argues that this law gives the government the power to exert stifling control over television programming. In Part II, Chapman contends that parents, rather than the government, should be responsible for monitoring children's exposure to television violence. Thierer is Walker Fellow in Economic Policy at the Heritage Foundation, a conservative think tank in Washington, D.C. Chapman is a nationally syndicated columnist.

As you read, consider the following questions:

1. What problems does Thierer believe will occur if the government creates a commission to rate television programs?
2. Why did the Fairness Doctrine have a chilling effect on free speech, according to Thierer?
3. How can parents control what their children see on television, according to Chapman?

Adam Thierer, "Enlisting Uncle Sam as a V-Chip Censor," *Washington Times*, July 30, 1995. Reprinted by permission of the author. Stephen Chapman, "V-Chip Asks Washington to Do the Thinking for Us," *Conservative Chronicle*, July 26, 1995. Reprinted by permission of Stephen Chapman and Creators Syndicate.

I

Advocates of a bill to require all televisions to carry the "V-Chip" portray the innovation as parents' ultimate weapon against television violence. In truth, the bill [which was signed into law in February 1996 as part of the Telecommunications Competition and Deregulation Act] hands your television's remote control to Washington bureaucrats.

The Violence Chip is not a new idea. The government tried, unsuccessfully, to control the content of programming with the "Fairness Doctrine" for 40 years, and failed. The V-Chip is just the latest approach—this time a technological one—that would give parents the ability to block violent or otherwise objectionable programming from being televised in their homes within sight of their children.

There certainly is nothing wrong with private-sector commercial cable systems selling this device to parents who wish to purchase it. Worried parents then would have the means—free of government monitoring or intrusion—to ensure healthy viewing by their children.

New Ratings System

But the bill goes way beyond such a sensible approach. As if mandating every new television set sold in America be equipped with the V-Chip weren't bad enough, the bill decrees creation by the entertainment industry of a new ratings system to govern what is shown on television and when.

If the new ratings system doesn't satisfy Congress, a new presidentially appointed federal Television Ratings Commission will draw up its own ratings. There is even talk in Congress of creating government-funded "TV Report Cards" for grading the quality of network programming.

The problems with this approach are numerous. First, how is a five-member commission going to rate every program available on television? By hiring a vast new staff of federal bureaucrats to monitor them, of course. Do you trust federal bureaucrats to distinguish properly between the horror of a documentary on the Holocaust and the gore in the film "Natural Born Killers"? What's to stop three of the five federal television ratings czars from deciding "The Rush Limbaugh Show" represents hateful speech that encourages violence, or from making other politically motivated rulings?

Fortunately, we need only look to recent history to see what happens when the government wields the power to censor entertainment. "Empowering" the audience was the harmless-sounding purpose for the Fairness Doctrine when it was introduced in 1949.

Under the Fairness Doctrine, the Federal Communications

Commission (FCC) required licensed broadcasters to air conflicting views on issues of public importance. The more viewpoints the better, the FCC reasoned. But that isn't exactly how things worked out.

Fearing loss of their FCC licenses if they were found to be in "noncompliance," broadcasters exercised prior censorship to exclude controversial materials. If they thought airing a program might require them to give equal time to an alternative viewpoint, many would opt not to air the original program at all. Thus, the Fairness Doctrine had a chilling effect on free speech. That's why the Reagan administration abandoned it in 1987.

Bureaucratic Report Card

Now we're being asked to support the V-Chip and the idea of federal bureaucrats carrying around report cards and rating television shows. Of course, it's only a rating system, advocates say. It wouldn't have any coercive power.

But in practice the V-Chip legislation empowers bureaucrats to govern via "the raised eyebrow," as one federal judge put it. That is, the mere threat of federal action would compel some broadcasters to carry programming they don't want and to exclude programming they might otherwise air, just as it did under the Fairness Doctrine. This definitely opens the door to control of TV programming by the federal bureaucracy. Is this what Americans want?

The American people understand the problems associated with grand bureaucratic schemes and are tired of Washington taking over their role as parental guardian. The nanny state is dying, but sneaky attempts—couched in pro-family rhetoric—are still being made to revive it.

The V-Chip is one of them. It should be stopped.

II

Sen. Kent Conrad, the North Dakota Democrat behind legislation to require a *V-chip* in every TV to block offensive programs, insists that "parents are increasingly unhappy that they have limited ability to control what their children watch on television. . . . Parents are fed up with the fact that their children are likely to be exposed to 200,000 acts of violence, including 40,000 murders, by the age of 18."

Well, of course they are. It is extremely frustrating to be hogtied, gagged and locked in a closet for hours every evening while your kids are madly channel-surfing through one scene of slaughter after another. Which is what must be happening to millions of parents if they are helpless to prevent Junior and Sis from personally witnessing 40,000 televised murders during their brief journey through childhood.

If parents are truly concerned about what their children see on the tube, they have lots of options. They can get rid of the TV. They can limit their kids' viewing hours. They can monitor the programs they watch. They can avoid subscribing to cable channels that offer too much flesh or too much blood.

They can also get devices, universally offered by cable TV operators for free or at a nominal cost, to darken individual channels for specified times. How many current subscribers order these gadgets from their cable companies? The National Cable Television Association says "very few." Conrad is demanding a new, government-imposed method of controlling what our children see when we are not using the highly effective ones already available.

Reprinted by special permission of North America Syndicate, Inc.

He cites a *USA Weekend* survey—which didn't pretend to use scientific methods—showing that 90 percent of Americans want the V-chip, with 83 percent supporting a ratings system for TV programs like that for movies. But a scientifically valid *Time/CNN* poll found that 69 percent also oppose government censorship to reduce sex and violence on the tube, with 81 percent preferring "voluntary self-restraint by entertainment companies" and 93 percent favoring "tighter parental supervision."

Censorship

Conrad's legislation, which was endorsed by President Clinton after it passed the Senate, involves as much censorship as self-control. It would force manufacturers of TV sets to build in a special electronic device, which would read a rating signal that broadcasters would presumably have to transmit with each program. So if you wanted to block all violent shows, regardless of channel or time of day, the V-chip would do it.

The bill gives broadcasters a year to come up with a ratings system, but if they decline, the Federal Communications Commission will do it for them—categorizing each program that goes out over the airwaves for violence, nudity and language. Each show would come with a government seal of approval—or a government message that it is "objectionable." Unlike movie ratings, which are voluntary and handled entirely without federal pressure, this one would be mandatory, with bureaucrats decreeing what is offensive and what is not.

As Washington civil-liberties lawyer Robert Peck writes, "Rating some television programs as violent or objectionable certainly places a pejorative label on them and, through the mechanism of the blocking device, substantially narrows their potential audiences." The V-chip legislation "may only be seen as facilitating the suppression of governmentally disfavored speech and thus is subject to constitutional attack." Imagine a McCarthy-era law rating shows for communist sympathies, and you see the problem.

The bill concocts a heavy-handed government solution to a problem already being addressed by the private sector. Broadcasters, TV manufacturers and cable operators, who have every interest in accommodating dissatisfied parents, have been working on a voluntary rating system of their own for years. The Electronic Industries Association says legislation will mean putting these plans on hold for months or years, until the courts rule on the constitutionality of the government mandate.

The problem, incidentally, is greatly exaggerated. Conrad and Clinton have somehow failed to notice that TV mayhem is not waxing but waning. . . .

What the Nielsen ratings demonstrate is that Americans are perfectly capable of controlling what they and their children watch without the interference of federal employees determined to sanitize the airwaves. The kids who are gorging on dreck have parents who aren't trying very hard to stop them. Before they start ministering to the rest of us, they ought to try healing themselves.

Periodical Bibliography

The following articles have been selected to supplement the diverse views presented in this chapter. Addresses are provided for periodicals not indexed in the *Readers' Guide to Periodical Literature*, the *Alternative Press Index*, the *Social Sciences Index*, or the *Index to Legal Periodicals and Books*.

Ken Auletta	"The Electronic Parent," *New Yorker*, November 8, 1993.
Brandon S. Centerwall	"Our Cultural Perplexities (V): Television and Violent Crime," *Public Interest*, Spring 1993.
David Cole	"Playing by Pornography's Rules: The Regulation of Sexual Expression," *University of Pennsylvania Law Review*, November 1994.
Barbara Dority and John Perry Barlow	"Ratings and the V-Chip," *Humanist*, May/June 1996.
Todd Gitlin	"The Symbolic Crusade Against Media Violence Is a Confession of Despair," *Chronicle of Higher Education*, February 23, 1994. Available from 1255 23rd St. NW, Suite 700, Washington, DC 20037.
Richard D. Heffner	"Here Come the Video Censors," *New York Times*, May 1, 1994.
Irving Kristol	"Children, Hollywood, and Censorship," *American Enterprise*, September/October 1995.
Fonda M. Lloyd	"Does Censorship Make Business Sense? Inner City Broadcasting Has Joined the Battle Against Violence in Music," *Black Enterprise*, May 1994.
Barry W. Lynn	"The Religious Right and Censorship: Just the Facts Ma'am," *Church and State*, April 1995. Available from AUSCS, 8120 Fenton St., Silver Springs, MD 20910.
Kyle E. Niederpruem	"It's Not a Matter of Decency, It's Just Censorship: Communications Act Threatens Free Speech," *Quill*, April 1996. Available from PO Box 77, Greencastle, IN 46135-0077.
Nils Gunnar Nilsson	"Children and Violence on the Screen," *UNESCO Courier*, February 1996.
Gary D. Schmidt	"Is This Book Safe?" *Education Digest*, October 1994.
Daniel T. Wackerman	"God Forbid That Anything Remotely Lewd or Gratuitously Violent Should Appear on the Old Zenith," *America*, March 2, 1996.

For Further Discussion

Chapter 1

1. In his viewpoint favoring a constitutional ban on flag burning, Paul Greenberg contends that the law should teach respect to a "less-than-civil society." Jeffrey P. Kaplan, on the other hand, argues that the First Amendment exists to "guarantee communication." Which of these two assertions do you find most compelling? Why? Is it more important for laws to protect rights or to teach civility? Explain your answer.

2. Nat Hentoff maintains that sexual harassment regulations have had a chilling effect on speech on American college campuses. However, George Rutherglen finds such laws to be "surprisingly moderate" and uncontroversial. Which writer makes a better case for his point of view? Support your answer with examples from the viewpoints.

3. L. Brent Bozell III argues against public funding of the arts because of the cost to taxpayers and because he thinks it is not the government's responsibility to control the arts. How does Hillary Rodham Clinton respond to these assertions? What does she see to be the long-term value of public funding? Which argument do you believe is more persuasive? Why?

Chapter 2

1. Many people argue that when an official removes a book from a school library in response to parental objections, it is an instance of book banning. Others insist that such an action does not constitute banning. Based on your reading of the viewpoints by Michael Granberry and Thomas Sowell, how do you define book banning?

2. Based on your reading of the first four viewpoints in this chapter, do you believe that censorship constitutes a significant obstacle to public education? If so, is the greatest threat from the right or from the left? Support your answer with references to the viewpoints.

3. Patrick M. Garry and Lawrence White agree that the purpose of campus speech codes is to protect individuals against offensive verbal expressions. However, Garry contends that such codes only drive prejudice underground and undermine free speech, which he believes to be an important aspect of college life. Do you believe it is more important to protect individuals from verbal assault or to protect the right of free speech regardless of its offensiveness? Explain your answer.

Chapter 3

1. Matthew S. Queler argues for stronger child pornography laws to protect children. However, Amy Adler and Marjorie Garber maintain that such laws would not have their intended effect. What results do Adler and Garber project for such laws? Which viewpoint is more persuasive? Why?

2. Jim Exon argues that government regulations can protect children from pornography on the Internet. Gary Chapman contends that due to the nature of the new computer technology such regulations will be largely ineffective. Whose viewpoint is more convincing? Why?

Chapter 4

1. Richard Zoglin offers numerous examples of excessive televised violence and cites studies linking such violence to antisocial behavior. Adam Thierer and Stephen Chapman, on the other hand, while not disputing the instances of violence, argue that any attempt by the government to control televised violence would be ineffective and would have a harmful effect on free speech. Do you believe violence should be restricted on television? If so, who should oversee the restrictions? What harmful side effects, if any, would result from such regulation?

2. After reading this chapter, present at least two arguments both for and against censorship of the entertainment media. Base your arguments on specific viewpoints from the chapter.

Organizations to Contact

The editors have compiled the following list of organizations concerned with the issues debated in this book. The descriptions are derived from materials provided by the organizations. All have publications or information available for interested readers. The list was compiled on the date of publication of the present volume; names, addresses, phone and fax numbers may change. Be aware that many organizations take several weeks or longer to respond to inquiries, so allow as much time as possible.

Accuracy in the Media (AIM)
1275 K St. NW, Suite 1150
Washington, DC 20005
(202) 371-6710

AIM is a conservative watchdog organization. It researches public complaints on errors of fact made by the news media and requests that the errors be corrected publicly. It publishes the bimonthly *AIM Report* and a weekly syndicated newspaper column.

American Civil Liberties Union (ACLU)
132 W. 43rd St.
New York, NY 10036
(212) 944-9800

The ACLU champions the rights set forth in the Declaration of Independence and Constitution. It opposes the censoring of any form of speech. The ACLU publishes the quarterly newsletter *Civil Liberties Alert* and several handbooks, public policy reports, project reports, civil liberties books, and pamphlets, including one on the Freedom of Information Act.

American Enterprise Institute for Public Policy Research (AEI)
1150 17th Ave. NW
Washington, DC 20036
(202) 862-5800

AEI is a conservative think tank whose resident scholars include Jeane J. Kirkpatrick and Robert Bork. AEI studies such issues as government regulation, religion, philosophy, and legal policy. The institute believes that the media are liberally biased and should be closely monitored. AEI's publications include books as well as the bimonthly magazine the *American Enterprise*.

American Library Association (ALA)
50 E. Huron St.
Chicago, IL 60611
(312) 944-6780

The ALA supports intellectual freedom and free access to libraries and library materials through its Office for Intellectual Freedom. ALA's sister organization, the Freedom to Read Foundation, provides legal defense in important First Amendment cases involving libraries' rights to acquire and make available materials representing all points of view. The ALA publishes the *Newsletter on Intellectual Freedom*, pamphlets, articles, posters, and the annually updated Banned Books Week Resource Kit.

Cato Institute
1000 Massachusetts Ave. NW
Washington, DC 20001
(202) 842-0200
fax: (202) 842-3490

The institute is a libertarian public policy research foundation dedicated to promoting limited government, individual political liberty, and free-market economics. It publishes the bimonthly *Policy Report* and the periodic *Cato Journal*.

Eagle Forum
Box 618
Alton, IL 62002
(618) 462-5415

The forum is a Christian group that promotes morality and traditional family values as revealed in the Bible. It opposes the depiction of sex and violence in the media. The forum publishes the monthly *Phyllis Schlafly Report* and the periodic *Newsletter*.

First Amendment Congress
1445 Market St., Suite 320
Denver, CO 80202
(303) 820-5688

The First Amendment Congress believes that a free press is not the special prerogative of journalists but a basic right that assures a responsive government. It works to establish a dialogue between the media and citizenry across the country, to encourage better education in schools about the rights and responsibilities of citizenship, and to obtain broader support from the public against all attempts by government to restrict citizens' right to information. It publishes the *First Amendment Congress Newsletter*, brochures, booklets, and educational materials.

Fund for Free Expression
485 Fifth Ave.
New York, NY 10017
(212) 972-8400

The fund is an organization of journalists, writers, editors, publishers, and concerned citizens who work to preserve freedom of expression throughout the world. It serves as the U.S. sponsor for the British pub-lication *Index on Censorship*, which reports violations of free expression worldwide. Its publications include *Off limits: Censorship* and *Corruption and Restricted Subjects: Freedom of Expression*.

The Heritage Foundation
214 Massachusetts Ave. NE
Washington, DC 20002
(202) 546-4400

The foundation is a public policy institute dedicated to the principles of free, competitive enterprise, limited government, individual liberty, and a strong national defense. It believes national security concerns jus-tify limiting the media. The foundation publishes a weekly bulletin, *Backgrounder*; a monthly journal, *Policy Review*; and many books and re-search papers. It has published as part of its Heritage Lecture Series a paper entitled "Why National Security Concerns and the First Amend-ment Are Not Compatible."

Morality in Media
475 Riverside Dr., Suite 239
New York, NY 10115
(212) 870-3222
fax: (212) 870-2765

Morality in Media opposes what it considers to be indecent material in broadcasting—especially pornography. It works to educate and organize the public in support of strict decency laws and has launched an an-nual "turn off the TV" day to protest offensive television programming. It publishes the *Morality in Media Newsletter* and the bimonthly *Obscen-ity Law Bulletin*.

National Coalition Against Censorship (NCAC)
275 Seventh Ave., 20th Fl.
New York, NY 10001
(212) 807-6222
fax: (212) 807-6245

NCAC opposes censorship in any form, believing it to be against the First Amendment right to freedom of speech. It works to educate the public about the dangers of censorship, including censorship of vio-lence on television and in movies and music. The coalition publishes *Censorship News* five times a year and various reports, such as "The Sex Panic: Women, Censorship, and 'Pornography.'"

National Coalition for the Protection of Children and Families
800 Compton Rd., Suite 9224
Cincinnati, OH 45231
(513) 521-6227

Formerly known as the National Coalition Against Pornography, the coalition is an organization of business, religious, and civic leaders who work to eliminate pornography. It believes that there is a link between pornography and violence. It encourages citizens to support the enforcement of obscenity laws and to close down pornography outlets in their neighborhoods. Its publications include *Final Report of the Attorney General's Commission on Pornography*, *The Mind Polluters*, and *Pornography: A Human Tragedy*.

National Coalition on Television Violence
33290 W. 14 Mile Rd., Suite 498
West Bloomfield, MI 48322
(810) 489-3177

The coalition is an educational and research organization committed to decreasing the amount of violence on television and in films. It sponsors speakers and seminars and publishes ratings and reviews of films and television programs. The coalition produces reports, educational materials, and the *NCTV Journal*.

Parents Alliance to Protect Our Children
44 E. Tacoma Ave.
Latrobe, PA 15650
(412) 459-9076

The alliance supports traditional family values and advocates censorship in cases where it believes these values are being undermined. It supports the inclusion of Christian teachings in textbooks and the labeling of records that contain offensive lyrics. It publishes position papers, including "Censorship and Education" and "Ratings-Labels on Recordings and Videos."

PEN American Center
568 Broadway
New York, NY 10012
(212) 334-1660
fax: (212) 334-2181

The center is the American branch of a worldwide organization of poets and playwrights, editors and essayists, and novelists—PEN, for short. Its Freedom to Write Committee organizes letter-writing campaigns on behalf of writers across the globe who are censored and/or imprisoned. It publishes the quarterly *Newsletter* and *Freedom-to-Write Bulletin*.

People For the American Way (PFAW)
2000 M St. NW, Suite 400
Washington, DC 20036
(202) 467-4999

PFAW is committed to reaffirming the traditional American values of pluralism, diversity, and freedom of expression and religion. It is engaged in a media campaign to create a climate of tolerance and respect for diverse people, religions, and values. It distributes educational materials, leaflets, and brochures and publishes the annual *Attacks on the Freedom to Learn*.

World Press Freedom Committee
c/o The Newspaper Center
11660 Sunrise Valley Dr.
Reston, VA 22091
(703) 648-1000

The committee monitors freedom of the press on an international level. It speaks out against "those who seek to deny truth in news and those who abuse newsmen." It has numerous articles on censorship available, including "A Missing Agenda" and "A Free Press Means Better Development."

Bibliography of Books

Ellen Alderman and Caroline Kennedy — *In Our Defense: The Bill of Rights in Action.* New York: William Morrow, 1991.

Stephen Bates — *Battleground: One Mother's Crusade, the Religious Right, and the Struggle for Control of Our Classrooms.* New York: Poseidon Press, 1993.

George Beahm, ed. — *War of Words: The Censorship Debate.* Kansas City, MO: Andrews and McMeel, 1993.

Francis J. Beckwith and Michael E. Bauman, eds. — *Are You Politically Correct? Debating America's Cultural Standards.* Buffalo, NY: Prometheus Books, 1993.

Mary Caputi — *Voluptuous Yearnings: A Feminist Theory of the Obscene.* Lanham, MD: Rowman & Littlefield, 1994.

J.M. Coetzee — *Giving Offense: Essays on Censorship.* Chicago: University of Chicago Press, 1996.

Ronald K.L. Collins — *The Death of Discourse.* Boulder, CO: Westview Press, 1996.

Cynthia DiLaura Devore — *Kids and Media Influence.* Minneapolis: Rockbottom Books, 1994.

Jonathan W. Emord — *Freedom, Technology, and the First Amendment.* San Francisco: Pacific Research Institute for Public Policy, 1991.

Stanley Eugene Fish — *There's No Such Thing as Free Speech, and It's a Good Thing, Too.* New York: Oxford University Press, 1994.

Patrick Garry — *An American Paradox: Censorship in a Nation of Free Speech.* Westport, CT: Praeger, 1993.

Kent Greenawalt — *Fighting Words: Individuals, Communities, and Liberties of Speech.* Princeton, NJ: Princeton University Press, 1995.

Franklyn S. Haiman — *"Speech Acts" and the First Amendment.* Carbondale: Southern Illinois University Press, 1993.

Marjorie Heins — *Sex, Sin, and Blasphemy: A Guide to America's Censorship Wars.* New York: New Press, 1993.

Nat Hentoff — *Free Speech for Me—but Not for Thee: How the American Left and Right Relentlessly Censor Each Other.* New York: HarperPerennial, 1993.

Edward S. Herman	*Beyond Hypocrisy: Decoding the News in an Age of Propaganda.* Boston: South End Press, 1992.
Carl Jensen and Project Censored	*Censored: The News That Didn't Make the News and Why.* New York: Seven Stories Press, 1996.
Claudia Johnson	*Stifled Laughter: One Woman's Story About Fighting Censorship.* Golden, CO: Fulcrum, 1994.
Robert Wheeler Lane	*Beyond the Schoolhouse Gate: Free Speech and the Inculcation of Values.* Philadelphia: Temple University Press, 1995.
Walter Laqueur	*Breaking the Silence.* Hanover, NH: University Press of New England, 1994.
Val E. Limburg	*Electronic Media Ethics.* Boston: Focal Press, 1994.
Martin London and Barbara Dill	*At What Price? Libel Law and Freedom of the Press.* New York: Twentieth Century Fund, 1993.
Catharine A. MacKinnon	*Only Words.* Cambridge, MA: Harvard University Press, 1993.
Wendy McElroy	*XXX: A Woman's Right to Pornography.* New York: St. Martin's Press, 1995.
Media Institute	*Speaking Freely: The Public Interest in Unfettered Speech.* Washington, DC: Media Institute, 1995.
Arthur J. Mielke	*Christians, Feminists, and the Culture of Pornography.* Lanham, MD: University Press of America, 1995.
Newton N. Minow and Craig L. LaMay	*Abandoned in the Wasteland: Children, Television, and the First Amendment.* New York: Hill and Wang, 1995.
Paul Monette	*The Politics of Silence.* Washington, DC: Library of Congress, 1993.
Marcia Pally	*Sex and Sensibility: Reflections on Forbidden Mirrors and the Will to Censor.* Hopewell, NJ: Ecco Press, 1994.
Richard Peck	*The Last Safe Place on Earth.* New York: Delacorte Press, 1995.
Lucas Powe Jr.	*The Fourth Estate and the Constitution: Freedom of the Press in America.* Berkeley and Los Angeles: University of California Press, 1991.
Jonathan Rauch	*Kindly Inquisitors: The New Attacks on Free Thought.* Chicago: University of Chicago Press, 1993.
Henry Reichman	*Censorship and Selection: Issues and Answers for Schools.* Chicago: American Library Association, 1993.

Casey Ripley Jr., ed.	*The Media and the Public.* New York: H.W. Wilson, 1994.
Barry Sanders	*A Is for Ox: Violence, Electronic Media, and the Silencing of the Written Word.* New York: Pantheon Books, 1994.
Lynne Segal and Mary McIntosh, eds.	*Sex Exposed: Sexuality and the Pornography Debate.* New Brunswick, NJ: Rutgers University Press, 1993.
Jefferson P. Smith	*Ambition, Discrimination, and Censorship in Libraries.* Jefferson, NC: McFarland, 1993.
Rodney A. Smolla	*Free Speech in an Open Society.* New York: Knopf, 1992.
Adele M. Stan, ed.	*Debating Sexual Correctness: Pornography, Sexual Harassment, Date Rape, and the Politics of Sexual Equality.* New York: Delta, 1995.
Nadine Strossen	*Defending Pornography: Free Speech, Sex, and the Fight for Women's Rights.* New York: Scribner, 1995.
Cass R. Sunstein	*Democracy and the Problem of Free Speech.* New York: Free Press, 1993.
Samuel Walker	*Hate Speech: The History of an American Controversy.* Lincoln: University of Nebraska Press, 1994.

Index